The Secret Life of
THE ADDER
The Vanishing Viper

The Secret Life of
THE ADDER
The Vanishing Viper

NICHOLAS MILTON

White Owl
AN IMPRINT OF PEN & SWORD BOOKS LTD.
YORKSHIRE – PHILADELPHIA

First published in Great Britain in 2022 by
White Owl
An imprint of
Pen & Sword Books Ltd
Yorkshire - Philadelphia

Copyright © Nicholas Milton, 2022

ISBN 978 1 39901 816 6

The right of Nicholas Milton to be identified as author of this work has been asserted by him in accordance with the Copyright, Designs and Patents Act 1988.

A CIP catalogue record for this book is available from the British Library.

All rights reserved. No part of this book may be reproduced or transmitted in any form or by any means, electronic or mechanical including photocopying, recording or by any information storage and retrieval system, without permission from the Publisher in writing.

Typeset in 11/14 pts Cormorant Infant
by SJmagic DESIGN SERVICES, India.
Printed and bound in India by Replika Press Pvt. Ltd.

Pen & Sword Books Ltd incorporates the imprints of Pen & Sword Books Archaeology, Atlas, Aviation, Battleground, Discovery, Family History, History, Maritime, Military, Naval, Politics, Railways, Select, Transport, True Crime, Fiction, Frontline Books, Leo Cooper, Praetorian Press, Seaforth Publishing, Wharncliffe and White Owl.

For a complete list of Pen & Sword titles please contact

PEN & SWORD BOOKS LIMITED
47 Church Street, Barnsley, South Yorkshire, S70 2AS, England
E-mail: enquiries@pen-and-sword.co.uk
Website: www.pen-and-sword.co.uk

or

PEN AND SWORD BOOKS
1950 Lawrence Rd, Havertown, PA 19083, USA
E-mail: Uspen-and-sword@casematepublishers.com
Website: www.penandswordbooks.com

Contents

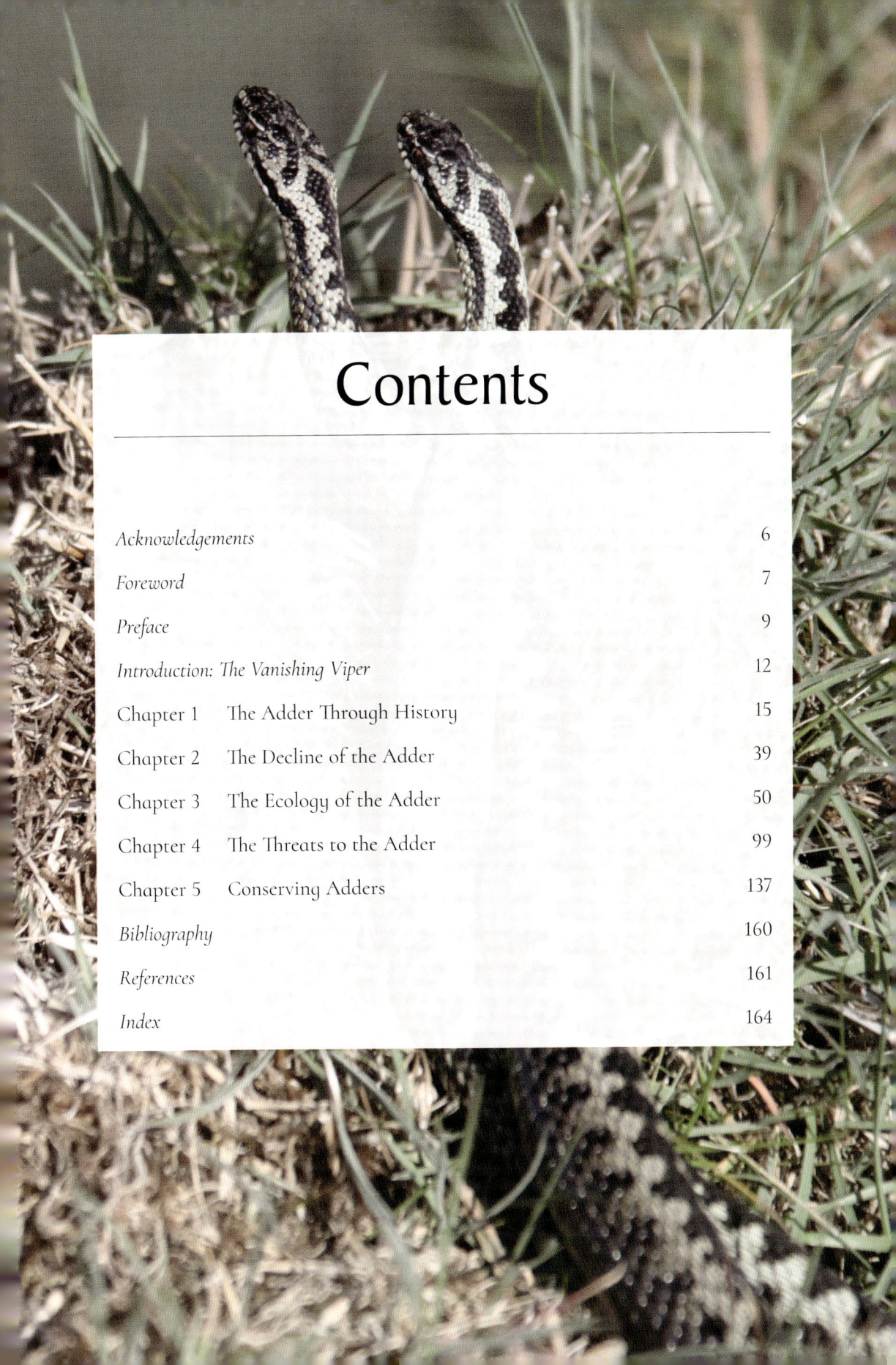

Acknowledgements 6

Foreword 7

Preface 9

Introduction: The Vanishing Viper 12

Chapter 1   The Adder Through History   15

Chapter 2   The Decline of the Adder   39

Chapter 3   The Ecology of the Adder   50

Chapter 4   The Threats to the Adder   99

Chapter 5   Conserving Adders   137

Bibliography 160

References 161

Index 164

Acknowledgements

I would like to thank Iolo Williams for writing the foreword to this book and for being such a great champion for adders in Wales and across Britain. Iolo and I worked at the Royal Society for Protection of Birds together back in the day and I am grateful for his support. This book benefitted from many interesting discussions and site visits with the herpetologist Nigel Hand. Nigel has spent much of his adult life studying the species and is an acknowledged expert on adders. I would also like to thank Roger McPhail who very generously donated to me so many of his adder pictures. Roger is a brilliant photographer and many of the images in this book are testimony to his skill and perseverance. Finally, this book is dedicated to the late Ian Prestt, a lovely man, who taught me so much about adders.

Foreword

I was four years old and my parents had taken us to the seaside at Trefdraeth on the north Pembrokeshire coast on a hot, late spring day. As a family, we'd spent most of the time on the beach or in the water but with a keen interest in wildlife from a very young age, I had begun to wander further afield to inspect the dunes and hedge banks. My mother warned me not to wander too far, a command that fell on deaf ears, but she needn't have worried because within a few feet of the edge of the sand, I had found my El Dorado, a female adder curled up amongst the marram grass.

Thousands of years of evolution has honed the human 'fight or flight' reaction to potential danger, but even as a very young child, common sense overcame instinct and I stood mesmerised as snake and human sized each other up. This stunning, bronze lady flicked her tongue out incessantly, the blood-red eyes fixed on this mini-human that dared trespass on her hunting grounds. She was an absolute beauty, of that there is no doubt, and from that day on my love of adders has never diminished.

Adders are probably our most misunderstood species. The fact that they are our only venomous reptile is a convenient fact bandied around by the bands of snake haters out there, ignorant people who make no effort to understand this enigmatic species. If I were given a pound for every time I've been told that 'a friend of a friend' had been set upon by a 6-foot adder I would be able to afford a cheap holiday to Torremolinos. My response to those who tell me that, unprovoked, they have been viciously bitten by an adder is to remark that I too would bite them if they shoved their fat, sweaty fingers in my face.

The truth is that for centuries, adders have been openly persecuted by humans and their habitats have diminished to such an extent that they are now considered functionally extinct over much of England and Wales. I'm very pleased to say, however, that times are changing and that an ever-growing army of enlightened adderphiles are appearing across the country to champion this species. Habitats are being restored and enhanced, children and adults alike are being educated and the adder is finally being appreciated for what it really is, a beautiful reptile that just wants to be left alone.

This book by Nick Milton has an important role to play in the education process, not just about the adder itself but also the measures that must be taken, and taken soon, to ensure its future. Losing the adder won't attract headlines like the demise of the lapwing or the hedgehog but it will be a damning indictment of us humans and our role on this planet.

Iolo Williams
Patron, The Amphibian and
Reptile Conservation Trust

Preface

Like a lot of young boys growing up, I was fascinated by snakes and spent hours searching for them in rough ground near my home. I can still vividly remember seeing my first adder coiled in the heather, a beautiful silver male with black zigzag markings down his back. I came across him while out exploring a local heath and on seeing the adder in front of me, I froze. Here was the animal I had read so much about, Britain's only venomous snake. It was one of those heart stopping moments, when time seems to stand still, and to this day I can still see him in my mind slowly slithering away.

After graduating with a degree in environmental studies, in 1990 I got my first job with the Royal Society for the Protection of Birds (RSPB). Apart from adders, birds were the other great love of my life and I was employed to carry our bird surveys on set-aside land. After the fieldwork season was over, I found myself working in the research department at their headquarters, the Lodge near Sandy, in Bedfordshire.

A magnificent male adder after it has sloughed its skin. The adder will be extinct across much of Britain in the next 15-20 years unless we act now to save it. (Nick Dobbs)

My job was to input the large amount of data generated by the project over the previous year. Unlike the fieldwork, it was a tedious and repetitive role which involved inputting lots of figures into an ancient computer. I soon became very bored and wished away the hours, often struggling to stay awake. One day, as a reminder of happier times, I pinned a sloughed adder skin above my desk.

A couple of weeks later, I was told that the RSPB's Director General, Ian Prestt, wanted to see me. I couldn't for the life of me think what he wanted and became convinced he was going to sack me. Ian had made his name working at the Nature Conservancy Council on the impact of pesticides on birds of prey. He had also worked in government where he was a special advisor to the Secretary of State for the Environment, Peter Walker MP, notable for being the world's first Environment Minister.

On entering Ian's big office, which overlooked the garden, to my surprise I found he was in a jovial mood having just seen a sparrow hawk, one of his favourite birds, land on the ledge of his window. After staring out over the garden for a while, he sat down and surprisingly asked me where I had got the snakeskin from above my desk. Instead of sacking me, Ian revealed he also liked adders and quizzed me on what I knew about them. Then, with a childlike grin on his face, he asked me if I'd like to go out with him to find some. Not believing my luck, I jumped at the chance.

I later learnt that Ian was being terribly modest about his interest in adders, which was very much in keeping with his quiet but determined personality. In fact, he had studied them for an MSc and in 1971 had published a pioneering paper in the *Journal of Zoology* called 'An ecological study of the viper *Vipera berus* in southern Britain.' Over the next six months, we went out once a week in my jalopy looking for snakes, travelling all over the Midlands and East Anglia in search of them. They were long days, but Ian always had the same boyish grin on his face and he never lost his sense of excitement whenever we found one. With every visit I learnt more about adders and the trips soon became the highlight of our week.

Our adder expeditions were always an adventure, on one occasion my old car breaking down miles from anywhere and leaving us stranded. On another occasion, Derek Ratcliffe came with us, one of the most knowledgeable ecologists of his generation and the Chief Scientist at the Nature Conservancy Council. It was early March, and the weather was bright but cold. As snow flurries came down, he and Ian got into a heated debate about whether adders would be out in such inclement conditions. Ian won after we found three adders out basking in a hollow on the heath.

As the weeks went by, I became aware that something was wrong with Ian's health. He would frequently be out of breath and struggled to walk long distances. But he always remained cheerful, often saying how good it was leave behind all the responsibility at the Lodge and escape into the field. I also found out more about him, learning on one visit that he had lost his only son in a tragic motorcar accident. Deep down I knew he was ill, but I never mentioned it and neither did he. Our visits were a chance to focus on our shared love of adders and to forget about the pressures at the Lodge.

In the winter of 1991, my contract with the RSPB came to an end and I moved away to become a farm conservation advisor. A couple of years later, I learnt that sadly Ian had died. His family kindly invited me to a memorial service in his honour which was held at St Paul's Cathedral. When I arrived, to my surprise, I sat at the front just behind his family, his widow Ann telling me how much he had enjoyed our visits.

I often wonder what Ian would have made of the decline of the adder across Britain in the thirty years since his death. What I do know is that he would have made the case for its conservation at the very highest level of government. And he would have quietly but determinedly kept pressing his case until they did something about it. In his absence, this book is my attempt to do exactly that – to wake up the government and its nature conservation agencies, the media and the public to its plight before it is too late.

A female adder after she has sloughed her skin. If we can save the adder, our children and grandchildren will inherit a countryside worthy of our generation. (Nick Dobbs)

INTRODUCTION

The Vanishing Viper

....*a serpent in the way, an adder in the path.*

Genesis 49:17

'It is the bright day that brings forth the adder. And that craves wary walking', wrote William Shakespeare in *Julius Caesar*. However, if he were alive today, the Bard would no longer have to be wary, as the adder has disappeared from his home county of Warwickshire and much of its former range across Britain. The bleak future facing our only venomous snake is that a creature which has been central to our culture from the time of the Bible could disappear in our lifetime.

In 2019, the most comprehensive survey ever of adders was published. According to 'Make the Adder Count', carried out by volunteers working for the Amphibian and Reptile Groups of the UK (ARG UK), the species will disappear from most of

Spot the adder. After emergence in the spring the adder's priority is to bask. (Author)

Britain in the next 15-20 years unless we take action now to save it. But despite being a priority conservation species under the UK Biodiversity Action Plan, not a single National Nature Reserve or Site of Special Scientific Interest has been specifically designated by the government to protect it.

Throughout our history, we have systematically persecuted the adder over generations because it is Britain's only venomous snake. Now the adder population is in dire straits, its rapidly declining numbers occurring on increasingly small, isolated and fragmented sites. According to Make the Adder Count, 90 per cent of the sites where it still occurs have ten or less adult snakes and are now considered to be very vulnerable to local extinction.

It is a sad fact that, despite being fully protected by law, adders are still killed illegally by people every year. However, many more are killed by predators like foxes, crows and particularly the millions of game birds which are released every year into the countryside. Disturbance is also a major problem, particularly by irresponsible dog walkers whose dogs can end up getting bitten, while there is increasing evidence that climate change and lack of genetic diversity is now also threatening adder populations.

When it comes to the media, no other species of British wildlife generates such unprovoked fear or lurid tabloid headlines as the adder. However, attitudes and times are slowly changing. There is now widespread acceptance that adders need our

Adders basking in the sun. Throughout our history, we have systematically persecuted the adder over generations because it is Britain's only venomous snake. (Ray Hamilton)

protection and that means giving them a fair press. Otherwise, when journalists come to write the epitaph of the adder, it will read like a Shakespearean tragedy of their own making.

The vanishing viper is a story of our times, one which typifies the age of extinction through which we are all living and for which we are all responsible. The conservation movement, particularly groups like ARG UK and The Amphibian and Reptile Conservation Trust, have done sterling work in raising the profile of the adder and monitoring the species. Yet for too long they have been fighting a losing battle to save it from local extinction at the sites where it still occurs.

Although the adder is on the verge of extinction across much of Britain, it is still not too late to save it if we act now. This is a ten-point adder action plan which if implemented could help to restore the adder population across Britain over the next decade.

1. Protect in law all remaining adder sites
2. Create viable adder populations in every county/region
3. Teach 'Adders are Amazing' in schools
4. Recruit a new generation of adder champions
5. Report sensational and negative adder stories to the press regulator
6. Expand the Back from the Brink projects to the whole of Britain
7. Ban dogs from all sites where adders occur
8. Make it illegal to release game birds within a mile of adder colonies
9. Build a nationwide network of adder corridors by rewilding
10. Designate adder nature reserves and fund a new adder conservation programme

Whether our children and grandchildren will see adders in the future now depends on us. It requires engaged politicians, inspired teachers, responsible news editors, enthusiastic champions, dedicated conservationists and sympathetic landowners to work together with the herpetological community to save it.

The UK government is rightly proud of being the first country in the world to produce a national Biodiversity Action Plan and to set a legally binding target to halt the loss of nature by 2030. However, it is also one of the most nature-depleted countries in the world. The adder is an indicator species of the health of our biodiversity, a barometer of how we treat the natural world. Save the adder and our children and grandchildren will inherit a countryside worthy of our generation.

CHAPTER 1

The Adder Through History

> The viper's tongue shall kill him.
>
> *Job 20:16*

When it comes to mysticism, myth and legend, there is no animal in Britain to rival the adder. Our only venomous snake, it has engendered fear and fascination throughout our history. With its zigzag stripe, red eye, elliptical pupil, forked tongue and fangs, the adder has played a prominent role in our folklore, literature and spiritual life for over 2,000 years.

The adder's ancestors first came to Britain when the country was still linked to mainland Europe as the last Ice Age retreated approximately 12,000 years ago. Venomous snakes along with many other animals were then spreading north as the tundra retreated but only the hardiest reptiles were able to survive Britain's climate. So it was just the adder among venomous snakes that colonised Britain, the species advancing all the way to the Arctic Circle, further north than any other snake in the world. However, one part of the British Isles remained uncolonized – Ireland. It had broken away from the mainland 2,000 years previously, the lack of snakes there much later giving rise to the legend of Saint Patrick.

From its first arrival, Britain's only venomous snake has been persecuted, killed and demonised. That record owes much to the snake's central role in the most read book in the world, the Bible. In the opening chapter, Genesis 3: 1-16, the serpent convinces Eve to eat fruit from the forbidden tree in the Garden of Eden, cutting off God from his chosen couple (see Box 1).[1] So God cursed the snake to crawl 'on its belly' and eat 'dust all the days of its life'. Snakes appear over fifty times in the Old and New testaments in the guise of serpents, asps, vipers and adders. Many references are oblique, but some clearly refer to species such as the Palestine viper *Daboia palaestinae* (see Box 2). Nearly all of them are to snakes being evil and biting, killing, poisoning or 'stinging'.

Yet, thousands of years before it became central to Christianity, the snake featured in a wide range of other cultures from the indigenous people of North America to the ancient Egyptians and Greeks (see Box 3). For these early people, far from symbolising evil, snakes represented fertility, rebirth, renewal and immortality.

An adder moves over rock. The adder is the only venomous snake to have reached Britain after the tundra retreated following the last Ice Age. (Roger McPhail)

Snakes feature prominently in the most read book in the world, the Bible. (Pixabay)

The asp or viper was a sign of royalty in ancient Egypt, Cleopatra famously committing suicide by enticing one to bite her arm. One of the oldest and most famous snake images in the world is the 'ouroboros' depicted on Tutankhamun's tomb which dates to the fourteenth century BC. A serpent devouring its own tail, it is an ancient symbol of life, death and rebirth and was probably a depiction of the Egyptian cobra *Naja haje*.

The first known records of adders in Britain are associated with the Druids, around 3BC, who believed they represented the rebirth of people, a symbolism associated with them shedding their skins and giving birth to live young. So highly valued were adders that the Druids kept them in captivity, basing key decisions on their movements. In Wales, the adder gave its name to an amulet worn around the neck called the Glein Neidr or 'adder's stone'. According to Welsh legend, adders joined together on Midsummer Eve to 'blow the stone', the amulet supposedly

The 'ouroboros' or serpent depicted on Tutankhamun's tomb is one of the oldest and most famous snake images in the world. (Djehouty)

warding off illness and helping the wearer look into the future. Like a lot of myths there is a grain of truth in it, adders producing a copious supply of saliva to help swallow their prey.[2]

Adders have long been associated with ancient cures and charms, the Anglo-Saxons believing dried snake skins could cure everything from headaches to blood disorders

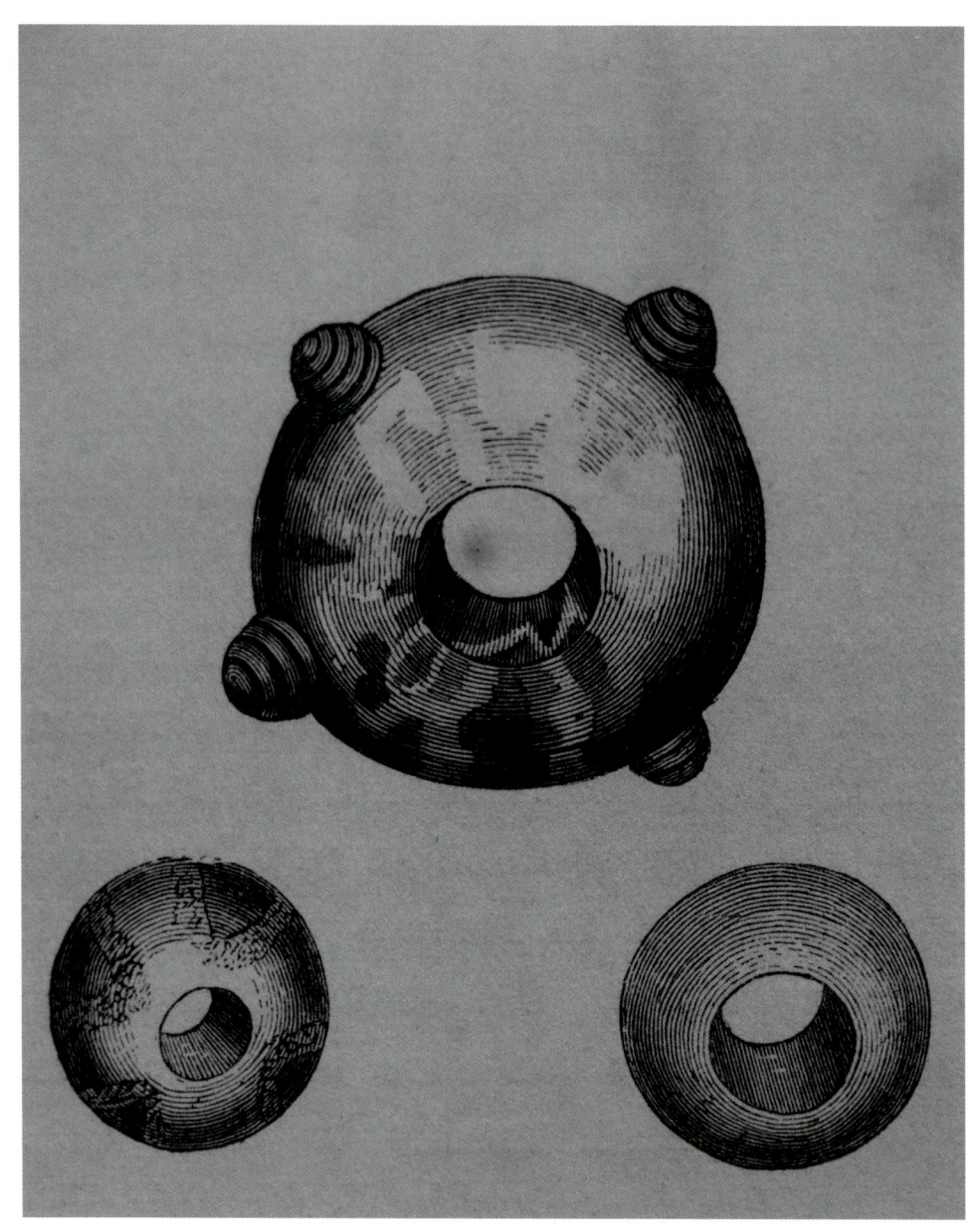

Adders' stones or 'glass of the serpents' was an amulet worn around the neck. Anglo-Saxons believed it cured illnesses and had mystic qualities. From Our Reptiles by M.C. Cooke published in 1865. (R. Hardwicke)

and when added to soup could alleviate constipation. Some of these so-called cures were still being practised into the early twentieth century, particularly in Wales where adders were revered. Adders were particularly associated with the Anglo-Saxon God Odin or Woden, most famous for being the origin of the word Wednesday. In the Old English medicinal poem *Nine Herbs Charm*, preserved in an eleventh century manuscript, he strikes an adder into nine pieces, mixing its venom with apple to ward off other snakes.

> *wyrm com snican, toslat he nan,*
> *ða genam woden VIIII wuldortanas,*
> *sloh ða þa næddran þæt heo on VIIII tofleah*
> *Þær gaændade æppel and attor*
> *þæt heo næfre ne wolde on hus bugan.*

> A snake came crawling, it bit a man,
> Then Woden took nine glory-twigs,
> Smote the serpent so that it flew into nine parts
> There apple brought this pass against poison
> That she nevermore would enter her house

The adder makes another appearance in the *De Proprietatibus Rerum* or 'On the Properties of Things' by the Franciscan monk Bartholomew Anglicus. Published in 1240 it was the encyclopaedia of the Middle Ages, the work running to 19 books, including one covering animals. In it, Bartholomew writes of a remedy for leprosy and a miraculous cure for blindness:

> .....to heal, or to hide leprosy, best is a red adder with a white womb, if the venom be away, and the tail and the head smitten off, and the body sod with leeks, if it be oft taken and eaten. And this medicine helpeth in many evils; as appeareth by the blind man, to whom his wife gave an adder with garlick instead of an eel, that it might slay him, and he ate it, and after that by much sweat, he recovered his sight again.[3]

The most famous legend associated with adders is that of Saint Patrick, the patron saint of Ireland. The story has it that the missionary rid Ireland of snakes as he converted its people from paganism to Christianity during the fifth century. During a 40-day fast on top of a hill, he supposedly chased the snakes into the sea after they began attacking him. The reality is that while adders are good swimmers and have colonised close islands like the Isle of Wight, the Irish Sea is too wide for them to cross. So Ireland remains one of only a handful of places in the world where there are no snakes, the others including New Zealand, Iceland, Greenland and Antarctica.

A male adder consumes a frog. In the Middle Ages the adder was believed to cure illnesses from leprosy to blindness. (Roger McPhail)

Saint Patrick famously chased all the snakes into the sea. While a myth, adders are good swimmers, but the Irish Sea was too wide for them to cross. (Junction City, Ohio)

The first record of an adder influencing British history dates to the sixth century where it played a part in the death of King Arthur, the legendary leader of the Knights of the Round Table. Arthur is supposed to have died in the Battle of Camlann in 537AD fighting against his treacherous illegitimate son Mordred (while most historians believe the legend of King Arthur is a myth, many battles did take place around this time). As the two armies faced each other across the battlefield, an adder suddenly emerged by Arthur's horse, one his men drawing his sword to kill it. Mordred seeing the sword being raised believed the battle had started and promptly charged, giving his army victory.

Some of the adder's most famous historical appearances are in the plays, poems and writings of Shakespeare. In *Macbeth* Act IV, Scene 1, written in 1606, the witches are preparing a spell so that Macbeth can see his future. Into the boiling cauldron are thrown:

> Eye of newt and toe of frog
> Wool of bat and tongue of dog
> Adder's fork and blind-worm's sting
> Lizard's leg and owlet's wing ...

The poisonous ingredients are all mixed together and a 'monster' created allowing Macbeth to see prophetic apparitions of his future. Shakespeare's mention of the adder's fork in the spell is a reference to the Adder's-tongue fern which resembles the snake's tongue, an image strongly associated with evil.

Mordred kills the legendary King Arthur in the Battle of Camlann. He had the advantage of surprise thanks to an adder suddenly appearing on the battlefield. (William Hatherell)

BOX 1: SNAKES IN THE BIBLE

In the opening chapter of the Bible in Genesis 3:1-16 the snake is chosen by Satan to bring about the fall, letting loose sin into the world. The passage begins:

> Now the serpent was more crafty than any of the wild animals the Lord God had made. He said to the woman, 'Did God really say, "You must not eat from any tree in the garden?"'
>
> The woman said to the serpent, 'We may eat fruit from the trees in the garden, but God did say, "You must not eat fruit from the tree that is in the middle of the garden, and you must not touch it, or you will die."'
>
> 'You will not certainly die,' the serpent said to the woman. 'For God knows that when you eat from it your eyes will be opened, and you will be like God, knowing good and evil.'
>
> When God learnt that it was the serpent that had deceived Eve into eating the forbidden fruit, He placed a curse on it for all time.
>
> Cursed are you above all livestock
> and all wild animals!
> You will crawl on your belly
> and you will eat dust
> all the days of your life.
> And I will put enmity
> between you and the woman,
> and between your offspring and hers;
> he will crush your head
> and you will strike his heel.

This is the first of over 50 references to snakes in the Bible, other synonyms for them including serpents, asps, vipers and adders. In the Old Testament the Hebrew word for snake is נָחָשׁ or nachash and in the New Testament the Greek word for snake is ὄφις or ofis. All these references to snakes demonise them with the exception of two.

In Matthew 10:16 Jesus tells his disciples to be 'wise like serpents', a reference to its 'crafty' nature mentioned in Genesis. 'See, I am sending you out like sheep into the midst of wolves; so be wise as serpents and innocent as doves.'

An alert adder blends in perfectly with the bracken. The words snake, serpent, asp, viper and adder are referred to over fifty times in the Bible. (Author)

In Numbers 21:4–8 God's wrath with the Israelites takes the form of sending venomous snakes to kill his disobedient and ungrateful people. To save them, Moses makes a bronze snake and puts it up on a pole, those looking at it being spared by God. Later speaking of this incident in the desert, Jesus says in John 3:14–15, 'Just as Moses lifted up the snake in the wilderness, so the Son of Man must be lifted up, that everyone who believes may have eternal life in him.'

Despite being used by Satan, most modern Christians now believe the association between snakes and evil to be figurative rather than literal. Nicky Gumblel, the evangelical vicar of Holy Trinity Brompton and the author of the Alpha Course, states 'A great deal of suffering can be explained as being the result of the fact that we live in a fallen world: a world where all creation has been affected, not only by the sin of human beings, but also before that by Satan's sin. [However], the serpent existed before Adam and Eve sinned.'[4]

Today, many Christians, far from demonising snakes, are part of the growing conservation movement and this is reflected in the increasing popularity of Christian environmental organisations like A Rocha and Operation Noah.

In Genesis 3: 1-16, the opening chapter of the Bible, it is the snake that convinces Eve to eat fruit from the forbidden tree in the Garden of Eden. (Brett Jordan)

The adder features prominently in the plays and poems of William Shakespeare. In Macbeth Act IV, Scene 1 into the boiling cauldron are thrown adder's fork and blind-worm's sting. (Mike)

Nearly two centuries later, adders featured in *The Natural History and Antiquities of Selborne*, one of our most celebrated natural history books, published in 1789. The renowned naturalist and parson Gilbert White came across one and, reflecting the times, killed it, writing:

> On August the 4th, 1775, we surprised a large viper, which seemed very heavy and bloated, as it lay in the grass basking in the sun. When we came to cut it up, we found that the abdomen was crowded with young, fifteen in number; the shortest of which measured full seven inches, and were about the size of full-grown earth-worms. This little fry issued into the world with the true viper-spirit about them, shewing great alertness as soon as disengaged from the belly of the dam: they twisted and wriggled about, and set themselves up, and gaped very wide when touched with a stick, shewing manifest tokens of menace and defiance, though as yet they had no manner of fangs that we could find, even with the help of our glasses [in fact adders are born with fangs].

A contemporary of White was William Augustus Osbaldiston, who included a herbal remedy for adder bites or 'Adder-stung' in his book *The British Sportsman, or Nobleman, Gentleman, and Farmer's Dictionary of Recreation and Amusement*, published in 1792. In it, Osbaldiston came up with an amazing herbal concoction for curing bites and some bizarre instructions for administering it.

THE SECRET LIFE OF THE ADDER

> THE
> # NATURAL HISTORY
> AND
> ## ANTIQUITIES
> OF
> # SELBORNE,
> IN THE
> ## COUNTY OF SOUTHAMPTON:
> WITH
> ## ENGRAVINGS, AND AN APPENDIX.
>
> ———   "ego Apis Matinæ
>   "More modoque
> "Grata carpentis ——— per laborem
> "Plurimum," ———————   Hor.
>
> "Omnia benè describere, quæ in hoc mundo, a Deo facta, aut Naturæ creatæ viribus
> "elaborata fuerunt, opus est non unius hominis, nec unius ævi. Hinc *Fauna* & *Flora*
> "utilissimæ; hinc *Monographi* præstantissimi."   SCOPOLI ANN. HIST. NAT.
>
> LONDON:
> PRINTED BY T. BENSLEY;
> FOR B. WHITE AND SON, AT HORACE'S HEAD, FLEET STREET.
> M,DCC,LXXXIX.

In The Natural History and Antiquities of Selborne, *Gilbert White wrote 'On August the 4th, 1775, we surprised a large viper......When we came to cut it up, we found that the abdomen was crowded with young, fifteen in number.' (B. White)*

   I. Garlic, onions, bacon and bay-salt, stamped together.
  II. Stamped rue, mustard seed, pickled herrings and black soap, with a sufficient quantity of deers suet and bear's grease.
 III. Cover the wound with Venice treacle or mithridate; either of them are very good, especially if the spiritous embrocations, used for gangrenes, be often used
 IV. Dragon's blood, barley-meal, and whites of eggs mixed to a thick consistence.[5]

By the beginning of the nineteenth century, the adder had become a great source of fascination for Victorian naturalists. To meet this demand in 1839 Thomas Bell, a Professor of Zoology at King's College London, published *A History of British Reptiles*. The book was one of the first widely accessible works which covered in detail all Britain's reptiles including the adder. Bell described it as being 'abundant in all parts of England and Wales, frequenting heaths, dry woods, and banks'. Interestingly, he also stated:

> It is everywhere deservedly feared on account of its venom, which, although less virulent than that of many other species, is yet sufficiently so to produce severe symptoms, and sometimes, in the warmer climates even fatal results. In this country I have never seen a case which terminated in death, nor have I been able to trace to an authentic source any of the numerous reports of such a termination, which have at various times been confidently promulgated.

Bell's painful remedy for an adder bite was 'the external application of oil, and the internal administration of ammonia'.[6]

Bell's book was followed in 1865 by the first pocket guide called *Our Reptiles – A plain guide and easy account of the Lizards, Snakes, Newts, Toads, Frogs and Tortoises indigenous to Great Britain* published by the naturalist Mordecai Cubitt Cooke. In it, he stated, 'In Scotland the Adder is common, whilst the Ringed Snake is but little known, and in

Adder from the first pocket guide to reptiles published in 1865 by the naturalist M.C. Cooke. 'I make no pretensions to the production of anything more than a popular volume on a rather unpopular subject.' (R. Hardwicke)

England and Wales it is as abundant as any could wish.' The book included 'original figures of every species', Cooke writing in the introduction:

> I make no pretensions to the production of anything more than a popular volume on a rather unpopular subject, to the espousal of the cause of a much-abused and scandalized class; and if I only aid in recovering their character from a little of the obloquy which attaches to them, I shall not regret the venture

It was not just in identification guides that adders appeared but also in fiction, in 1878 adders famously featured in Thomas Hardy's *The Return of the Native*. Set on Egdon Heath, a 'vast tract of unenclosed wild', the novel features an encounter between Mrs Yeobright and an adder which gives her 'the evil eye'. After leaving the home of Eustacia, her devious daughter-in-law, she suffers an adder bite on her foot during a walk on the heath. Mrs Yeobright is then carried by her son into a hut where locals from the heath gather around her bedside. One states that the only cure for an adder bite is to apply oil extracted from the fat of other adders. So three adders are brought into the hut, two already being dead, but the third is still 'briskly coiling and uncoiling in the cleft of the stick' used to carry it. Hardy then writes:

> The live adder regarded the assembled group with a sinister look in its small black eye, and the beautiful brown and jet pattern on its back seemed to intensify with indignation. Mrs Yeobright saw the creature, and the creature saw her: she quivered throughout, and averted her eyes

The author Anna West, who has studied Hardy's relationship with animals, believes the 'small black eye' of the adder is a metaphor for Eustacia's 'wild dark eyes' which were well known for their 'ill-wishing power'. She states:

> The superstitious suggestion of 'overlooking' and 'ill-wishing' – or the idea that the gaze has the potential to carry harm, whether intentional or accidental – does seem to connect Eustacia and the adder through the myth of the snake-haired Medusa, the figure perhaps most associated with the evil eye[7] (see Box 3).

By the time *The Return of the Native* was written, catching and killing adders had become a national past-time for those living near heaths, commons and woods. Two years after the book was published, the most famous snake catcher ever took up residence in the New Forest. In 1880, at the age of 40, Harry 'Brusher' Mills moved into an old charcoal burner's hut in the forest near to Brockenhurst. There he took up snake catching for a living armed with just a forked stick and a sack. Mills rid local people of 'problem snakes' and over the next 25 years killed thousands of snakes,

Adders famously appeared in the Thomas Hardy novel The Return of the Native *written in 1878. Mrs Yeobright is bitten by an adder, another then being brought to the hut which gives her 'the evil eye'. (Hardy)*

most of them adders. After killing them, he would make oil out of their bodies as an anti-venom or sell their skeletons to tourists. He even supplied both adders and grass snakes to London Zoo as prey for their snake-eating eagles. After a media article about him was published in a national paper, he became a local celebrity, tourists paying to have their photograph taken with him.

One person who met Mills was Adelaide Clarence Browne who wrote about him in *The Life-History of British Serpents and their Local Distribution in the British Isles,* by the herpetologist Gerald Leighton, in 1901:

> During the time we lived in the New Forest I was acquainted with the old snake-killer 'Brusher' whom I met one day when out walking. He was carrying his pouches full of writhing snakes. I asked him if he had found many adders, and said I should like to see him catch one, and told him I would help him to find one. We strolled to a likely spot, but 'Brusher' found the adder, and quickly whipping out his tongs, seized it near the head. 'Now, marm' said he, 'would you like to see its teeth?' 'Oh yes,' said I, and with the help of other tweezers he made the poor creature open its mouth wide, and I had a fine view … I said that I had heard that he made oil from adders that would cure their bite, whereupon he pulled out a bottle of clear oil from his pocket, and showed me the dreadful bites on his own hands he had cured with the oil. I asked him how he got the

oil, and with a grin he said that he baked the adders in an oven, in a large jar. 'Please marm,' said he, 'would you like to see this one have a run and me catch it again?'!!! But this was more than I had nerve for, and leaving the old man a small present, I made off as fast as I could.[8]

Harry 'Brusher' Mills was the last great snake catcher. From 1880, he lived in the New Forest and killed thousands of snakes, making oil out of their bodies as an anti-venom or selling their skeletons to tourists (W. Blackwood and Sons)

Apart from snakes, Brusher Mill's other great passion was cricket, he brushing the pitch between innings which gave rise to his nickname. In 1904, he built himself a larger hut in the forest but it was destroyed by vandals so that he could not claim squatters rights. Heartbroken, he took up residence in his local pub, the Railway Inn in Brockenhurst, where he proved extremely popular but died a year later. In remembrance, the locals clubbed together to pay for a marble headstone which stands to this day in the churchyard of St. Nicholas in Brockenhurst and in his honour the pub was renamed The Snakecatcher.

After the First World War, attitudes towards snakes slowly started to change as the fledgling conservation movement grew in influence. In 1919, the author William Henry Hudson wrote a remarkable book called *The Book of a Naturalist*, published by Hodder and Stoughton, in which he included a chapter called 'Hints to adder-seekers.'[9] Hudson was fascinated by adders and was quietly appalled that one so-called friend had offered sixpence to any of the boys in his village who brought him a dead grass snake or adder. Instead, his book made the case for their conservation by championing another friend who was a 'snake saviour' and instead offered sixpence for every snake they brought him alive. According to Hudson, to 'inspire confidence in them he would go with half a dozen large snakes in his coat pockets into the village school, and pulling his pets out, would play with and make the children handle them and take note of their beautiful form and motions'.

An adder before it has sloughed its skin. After the First World War attitudes towards snakes began to slowly change. (Author)

Hudson believed that many more people wanted to see adders alive rather than dead, 'seeing that there are very many persons desirous of making the acquaintance of this rare and elusive reptile. They wish to know it – at a safe distance – in a state of Nature, in its home, and have sought and not found it.' So Hudson published his hints for adder seekers stating 'not only must the seeker go softly, but he must have a quick-seeing, ever searching eye, and behind the eye a mind intent on the object.' Instead of killing adders, as he had done in his youth, Hudson instead urged his readers to study them, recounting a tale of how he had found one in the New Forest and captured it before letting it go. 'I fondly hoped to see it again many times' he wrote, 'I remember the finding of that adder as one of the loveliest experiences I have met with during all the years I have spent in conversing with wild animals.'

After the Second World War, the adder featured in the writing of the best-selling children's author Enid Blyton. In 1952, Blyton published the *Animal Lover's Book* in which two children, Richard and Susan Rennie, were introduced to a range of animals by the gipsy naturalist Zachary Bosell, who they nicknamed Zachy. In a chapter called 'In Snake Hollow' Zachy introduces them to the adder:

> Zachy took out his carved flute and put it to his lips. He blew, his fingers running up and down the holes in the flute, so that different notes came out....
> And then she saw the first snake! It came gliding out of the bushes, silent and

The adder's coloration provides it with superb cryptic camouflage. In 1919, William Hudson published a remarkable book called The Book of a Naturalist *including 'hints to adder-seekers' (Roger McPhail)*

wary. 'An adder' said Zachy quietly, out of the corner of his mouth and went on playing. The snake came up to his knee. Then Susan nearly gave a scream. It put out a long black tongue, that was deeply forked into two. Its tongue played over Zacky's brown hand, which rested now on his knee. 'Don't adders sting' whispered Susan, fearfully. 'Is that its sting?' The snake glided round Zachy's legs, and then coiled up by his feet. Zachy blew occasional notes on the flute, and answered in a low voice: 'Snakes don't have stings. They can only bite. This adder cannot sting - but he can bite. Don't be afraid. The music has charmed him – he is sleepy and happy. Look at him well. He is the only poisonous snake we have.'[10]

Although the book is of its time, perpetuating the myth that adders can hear and repeating the misnomer that they are poisonous (as opposed to venomous), Blyton was in her own way quite progressive when it came to her attitude towards snakes. Later in the chapter, Zachy brings down his hazel walking stick just in front of the snake to 'startle it wide awake' and show the children its fangs before it is allowed to silently glide away. In contrast, Brusher Mills would have brought his stick down on its head and killed the snake before skinning it.

Over a century has passed since Britain's last snake catcher died and half a century since Enid Blyton wrote 'In Snake Hollow', a period during which the adder population

The adder featured in the Animal Lover's Book by the children's author Enid Blyton. Published in 1952 it includes a chapter called 'In Snake Hollow'. (Camelot Press)

In Snake Hollow

behind me. That's right. I'm going to play my flute, and you must watch. I'll tell you what snake it is that comes first."

This was really very exciting. The two children sat down, and Silky sat beside them. He seemed to guess what Zacky meant to do. He put his head down on his paws and looked rather bored.

Zacky took out his carved flute and put it to his lips. He blew, his fingers running up and down the holes in the flute, so that different notes came out.

Richard had never heard anything like it. It was queer. He soon felt rather as if he were in a dream, listening to the deep, liquid notes playing the same little tune and rhythm time and time again. He shook his shoulders to wake himself up. Susan was listening intently, too.

"If I were a snake, I'd come," she thought. "The flute calls and calls."

And then she saw the first snake! It came gliding out of the bushes, silent and wary.

"An adder," said Zacky quietly, out of the corner of his mouth, and went on playing again. The snake came up to his knee. Then Susan nearly gave a scream. It put out a long black tongue, that was deeply forked into two. Its tongue played over Zacky's brown hand, which rested now on his knee.

"Don't adders sting?" whispered Susan, fearfully. "Is that its sting?"

The adder

Enid Blyton wrote 'And then she saw the first snake! It came gliding out of the bushes, silent and wary....Then Susan nearly gave a scream.' (Camelot Press)

An adder basks in the leaf litter. Over a century has passed since Britain's last snake catcher died, a period during which the adder population has crashed. (Author)

has crashed. Today even if it were legal no one could make a living catching adders or selling snake flutes but they continue to be feared and misunderstood, in no small part due to their portrayal in popular culture (see Box 7). So God's curse on the snake in the Bible was darkly prophetic, its demonisation continuing to this day in the guise of B-list movies and sensational news stories.

BOX 2: WHAT IS THE REAL ADDER IN THE BIBLE?

The word adder or viper in Hebrew is צִפְעוֹנִי or tsiphoni and it appears nine times on its own in the Bible. All the references to the adder or viper are of it biting, killing, poisoning or stinging.

Genesis 49:17 Dan will be a serpent in the way, an adder in the path, That bites the horse's heels, so that his rider falls backward.

Job 20:16 He shall suck cobra venom. The viper's tongue shall kill him.

Psalms 58:4 Their poison is like the poison of a serpent: they are like the deaf adder that stoppeth her ear.

Psalms 91:13 Thou shalt tread upon the lion and adder: the young lion and the dragon shalt thou trample under feet.

Psalms 140:3 They have sharpened their tongues like a serpent; adders' poison is under their lips. Selah.

Proverbs 23:32 At the last it biteth like a serpent, and stingeth like an adder.

Isaiah 11:8 The nursing child shall play over the hole of the asp and the weaned child shall put its hand on the adder's den.

Isaiah 14:29 Don't rejoice, O Philistia, all of you, because the rod that struck you is broken; for out of the serpent's root an adder will emerge, and his fruit will be a fiery flying serpent.

Isaiah 59:5 They hatch adders' eggs, and weave the spider's web: he who eats of their eggs dies; and that which is crushed breaks out into a viper

The European adder does not occur in the Middle East so what species were scholars referring to when they wrote about it in the Bible? In the modern day countries which make up the Bible lands, snakes are not especially abundant, Israel having 42 species including nine venomous ones. The most common snake in the area is the coin-marked snake *Hemorrhois nummifer* which can grow up to 1.5 metres in length. Sometimes mistaken for a viper because of the brown spots on its back, it is harmless to humans. One was even discovered in the holy Western Wall in Jerusalem where it lived in the crevices looking for mice and other prey. When worshippers saw it emerging from between the cracks one day, it caused panic and a professional snake-catcher had to remove it.

Michael Bright, a senior producer at the BBC Natural History Unit, has written extensively about animals in the Bible. He believes the term adder is used very ambiguously by biblical scholars and could refer to at least five different venomous species. Two candidates are the horned viper *Cerastes* (several species) or the false horned viper *Pseudocerastes* (several species). In Genesis 49:17 there is an adder in the path which bites the horse's heels. Both horned and false horned vipers bury themselves in sand with just their eyes, nostrils and horns present above the surface, where they wait to ambush passing prey such as mice, lizards and rodents. So the behaviour described in the passage sounds very like one of these species, the viper striking in defence after the horse disturbed it.

Other candidates are the ottomans or rock viper *Montiviper xanthina* and the blunt-nosed viper or kufi *Macrovipera lebetinus*. Occurring on rocky slopes and outcrops as well as gullies, gorges, river valleys, vineyards and orchards, both species would have been common in Biblical times. However, the most likely candidate for the majority of references to adders in the Bible is the Palestine viper *Daboia palaestinae*. Measuring up to 1.5 metres in length, it is endemic to the Levant or modern day Syria, Lebanon, Jordan, Israel, Palestine and south-eastern Turkey. Found close to human habitation including people's houses, the Palestine viper superficially resembles the European adder, but its venom is far more toxic to people.

In Hebrew it is known as the common viper or Land of Israel viper, the species being responsible for the overwhelming majority of snake bites in Israel and the West Bank. On average, around 300 people are bitten each year although deaths are extremely rare thanks to the widespread availability of a serum. The Palestine viper was given its Latin name *Daboia palaestinae* by the famous Austrian herpetologist Franz Werner in 1938 during the British Mandate over Palestine. In 2018, in a sign of changing attitudes towards snakes since Biblical times, it was officially declared as Israel's national snake in a public poll organised by the Society for the Protection of Nature in Israel and the Israel Nature and Parks Authority.

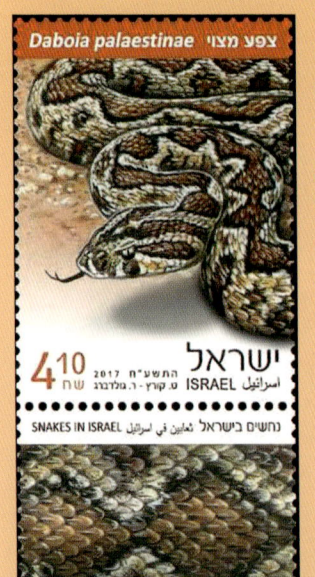

The Palestine or Land of Israel viper is one of the snake species referred to in the Bible. In 2018 in a sign of changing attitudes towards snakes Israel adopted the species as its national snake. (Israel Post)

CHAPTER 2

The Decline of the Adder

..... they are like the deaf adder that stoppeth her ear
Psalms 58:4

In the seminal 1901 book *The Life-History of British Serpents and their Local Distributions in The British Isles*, written by the herpetologist Gerald Rowley Leighton, there is a picture of the last great snake-catcher Brusher Mills sitting on a log.[1] Mills is sporting a long straggly beard and wearing his characteristic wide brimmed hat. His hands are full of writhing snakes which he is showing off for the camera with a big grin on his face. Mills had every reason to be happy as the adder was then a widespread species across England, Scotland and Wales, the New Forest where he lived being a particular stronghold. Leighton's book was not just another Edwardian nature book but was the first comprehensive survey of each 'serpent', the author collating the results of thousands of field naturalists around Britain and dedicating his book to them.

In the preface Leighton writes, 'That correspondence has been a source of very great pleasure to me....Without their cordial help my effort to compare our *Ophidia* [snakes] in various localities must necessarily have been barren of results.' However, Leighton also had an ulterior motive for undertaking the study – he was trying to prove the existence of a new adder species to science which if verified would have made his name as one of the great herpetologists of his era.

Leighton was born in 1868 in Blackpool, the son of James Leighton who was a missionary and clergyman. He was educated at Manchester Grammar school and then studied medicine at Edinburgh University, graduating in 1895 and specialising in animal health. However, Leighton's passion was reptiles and he would spend much of his spare time searching for them in the hills and valleys around his home. By the time he published his book on British serpents, Leighton had progressed to become Professor of Comparative Pathology and Bacteriology at the university's Royal Veterinary School.

To assess how common the adder then was across Britain and test his theory of a new species, Leighton enlisted 'the aid of field naturalists all over the land' and through them 'endeavoured to get a record of our serpents for every county in the kingdom'. His method of doing this was to write to the secretaries of all the Field

COMMON VIPER. 61

SQUAMATA.
(OPHIDIA.)

VIPERADÆ.

Genus, *Pelias*. Merr.

Generic Character.—Head depressed, oblong-ovate, somewhat compressed before, and wider behind the eyes; vertex covered with scuta; no pit between the nostrils and eyes; tail with double plates beneath.

COMMON VIPER.

ADDER.

Adder plate from the seminal book The Life-History of British Serpents and their Local Distributions in The British Isles *by the herpetologist Gerald Leighton in 1901. (W. Blackwood and Sons)*

Naturalists Clubs in all those counties 'where such societies are working'. In his letter, he asked the following questions:

1. Which snake is most common in the county (or district) of ....?
2. What is the average length of the adder here?
3. What is the average length of the ring snake (grass snake) here?
4. Does the smooth snake occur to your knowledge?
5. Does the small red viper occur?
6. Kindly add any other note on snakes you deem of interest.

Leighton was the leading protagonist of the theory that there were actually two adder species living in Britain at the time – the 'common adder' and the 'small red viper.' This was controversial even in 1901, most herpetologists believing 'small red vipers' were the young of the adder and changed colour as they matured. However, Leighton maintained that the small red viper was a separate species 'better known to those whose occupations take them to the haunts of snakes than to scientific naturalists' or in other words to field naturalists like himself rather than the established herpetological community.

To collate the results, Leighton divided each country into counties bordering rivers. For example, along the river Severn he noted the grass snake was the most common but

A male adder on the move. To assess how common the adder was across Britain at the start of the twentieth century Leighton enlisted 'the aid of field naturalists all over the land'. (Roger McPhail)

the adder still occurred in every county. In Gloucestershire he described the adder as 'plentiful' on the 'Cotteswolds' and in Monmouthshire it was the 'common serpent' in the north of the county. In Herefordshire, the adder was widespread and so were many of the legends about it, Leighton commenting 'The belief that the adder-mother swallows her young is prevalent throughout the county, and I must have had the incident described to me by quite fifty people who said they witnessed it. But I am still waiting for the specimen with the young in the gullet' (See box 5). In Worcestershire, the adder was local but common in the Wyre Forest, in Warwickshire it was described as being fairly common a few miles from Birmingham and in Staffordshire it was found on 'Cannock Chase and Chartley Park, Whitmore and Wybunbury.' In Shropshire it was 'fairly numerous in the neighbourhood of Oswentry and Ellesmere, on Rudge Heath and Whixall Moss in the north, and on Titterstone Clee Hill and in the Forest of Wyre in the south.'

Nationally the results of Leighton's survey showed that, despite nearly 2,000 years of persecution, the adder had maintained its range, if not its former abundance, and that throughout Britain there were many strongholds where the species was either holding its own or increasing. However, what the survey did reveal for the first time was how locally distributed the adder was, Leighton concluding this was 'a striking feature of British serpents, and is to be noticed in many counties. People who live on different sides of the same range of mountains, though perhaps in the same county, may make directly opposite statements as to which serpent is the most common, and both are probably right.'

A juvenile adder. Leighton believed there were two adder species living in Britain – the 'common adder' and the 'small red viper' but his theory was dismissed. (Nick Dobbs)

When it came to the small red viper, Leighton was delighted to find that it was recorded in 15 counties 'where the ordinary adder is also found, though the two differ greatly in size as well as in appearance'. In the Severn Province, that included the north of Monmouthshire and Garaway Hill in Herefordshire. Leighton felt vindicated by the survey and was convinced that the reporting of the small red viper in so many counties confirmed his hypothesis. However, on publication of his book in 1901 the herpetological and scientific community remained unconvinced and dismissed his theory. One critic reviewing the book in *Nature* magazine wrote 'It is only regrettable that Dr. Leighton, whilst engaged in the preparation of this little work, which contains much interesting matter, should not have made himself more thoroughly acquainted with what has been published on the subject... and this is all the more to be regretted since many points of structure and coloration which are subject to variation would have afforded an important topic in which to arouse the interest of the field-naturalist.'

After the publication of Leighton's book, there was no debate about the small red viper and he never got to name a new adder species to science. However, the following year he did have a snake named after him, the Cape sand snake *Psammophis leightoni* (Leighton presented a specimen to the British Museum following a field trip to South Africa) and he founded the *Field Naturalists Quarterly* magazine where he continued to promote his ideas. His career also flourished, the next year Leighton receiving his doctorate and being elected as a Fellow to the Royal Society of Edinburgh. In 1903 he

A male adder guards a female. Leighton's 1901 survey of the adder marks a defining point in the species' distribution and gives a good indication of how common the adder once was. (Roger McPhail)

published a follow up book, *The Life-History of British Lizards*, and went on to publish several more books. Leighton served as a Lieutenant Colonel in the Royal Army Service Corps during the First World War and died on the Isle of Man in 1953.

Leighton's survey of the adder in 1901 marks a defining point in the species' distribution and though by no means comprehensive, it gives a good indication of how common it once was. The adder continued to be a widespread, if localised, species up to the mid-1930s, after which biological recording data submitted by local naturalists began to indicate a decline in its numbers.[12] This was caused in part by the large pre-war house building programme instigated by the Chancellor Neville Chamberlain as a way of stimulating the economy following the global recession. The result was the mass building of semi-detached homes around London and across southern England, between the wars over four million new homes being constructed. Many of these were on heaths or on the edge of existing towns, their building resulting in the destruction of many adder colonies.

In 1939 with the outbreak of the Second World War, the famous Dig for Victory campaign was launched by the Ministry of Agriculture. The campaign resulted in many open spaces, including commons, parks and 'waste land' containing adder colonies being brought into cultivation or turned into allotments. After the war, the destruction of wildlife habitats continued apace as new towns sprang up across Britain to relocate people in poor or bombed out housing. Post-war agriculture policy also continued to bring more marginal land back into production as successive governments tried to ensure Britain became more self-sufficient in food production. However, it was Britain joining the European Economic Community in 1973 and its Common Agricultural Policy which precipitated the steepest decline in adder habitats as large areas of heath, commons and scrub were ploughed up by farmers in response to new economic subsidies and quotas. The result was the whole scale destruction of many adder sites, especially in lowland England, while in the uplands of Scotland and Wales, intensive sheep farming and moorland management for driven grouse shooting had a similar impact.

By the 1980s, adder declines were being detected across Britain by local naturalists, but the lack of a national survey meant that the overall picture remained unclear and the level of decline difficult to assess. In order to get a more accurate picture, a questionnaire was sent out by the Nature Conservancy Council in 1983 which recorded declines in three out of its 12 regions[13] (the NCC was the government body responsible for nature conservation, set up in 1973 it divided Britain into regions composed of several counties). A follow-up survey was carried out in 1991, which found that adder populations were now declining across half of Britain, reductions being recorded in six out of the 12 regions.[14]

By now the plight of the adder was becoming of increasing concern to conservationists and so in 2004 another study was carried out at specific

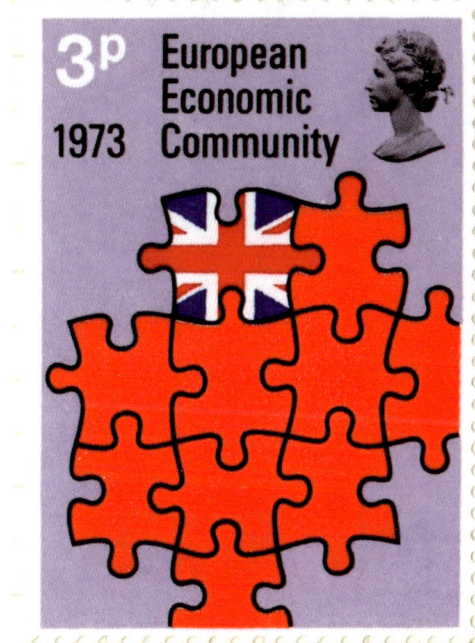

Above left: In 1939 with the outbreak of the Second World War, the famous Dig for Victory campaign was launched by the Ministry of Agriculture destroying many adder colonies. (Ministry of Information)

Above right: Britain joining the European Economic Community in 1973 and its Common Agricultural Policy precipitated the steepest decline in adder numbers as farmers destroyed habitats in response to new economic subsidies and quotas. (Royal Mail)

adder sites. This again used a questionnaire and recorded that most populations were decreasing with the most significant declines being found in the Midlands.[15] In 2012, another study found that across its range the adder had declined by 39 per cent, a figure calculated by combining historical records with the amount of suitable habitat left where adders could occur.[16] The adder was clearly in trouble but without a proper national survey, based on a recognised recording method rather than questionnaires or ad hoc site studies, it was impossible to quantify. The answer finally came in 2019, thanks to citizen science and the results shocked even experienced herpetologists.

In 2005 the Amphibian and Reptile Groups of the UK (ARG UK) launched Make the Adder Count, a citizen science survey to monitor adder populations across Britain (see Box 8). The survey was carried out using volunteer surveyors with experience of reptile fieldwork who were asked to visit their local adder sites and count the numbers of animals to record if populations were increasing or decreasing. As adders are a relatively sedentary species which use the same hibernacula every year, the volunteers counted the number of basking adders found close to hibernation sites in the spring.

Surveyors made a minimum of three visits to sites between February and May and were asked to do so in optimum weather conditions i.e. on sunny days when adders are basking, both adult male and female snakes being recorded.

From 2005 to 2016, 181 surveyors provided information on 260 sites spread throughout Britain and found a peak count of 848 snakes with 768 occurring on small sites and 80 on large ones. As a result of the number of surveyors taking part and the rigorous methodology, Make the Adder Count was the most comprehensive survey ever undertaken of the species in Britain. The monitoring data was analysed in 2016 by Dr Emma Gardner, a researcher from the University of Reading in conjunction with three members of the ARG UK – Angela Julian, Chris Monk and John Baker – and the results were published in *The Herpetological Journal* in 2019. The shocking headline was that the adder could disappear from much of the countryside in the next 15-20 years, a devastating indictment of our ability to conserve a species which has played such a prominent part in our folklore and history. The survey, which was the culmination of 11 years of recording by adder enthusiasts up and down Britain, also showed that 90 per

A male adder guards a female. Make the Adder Count was the most comprehensive survey of the species ever undertaken. (Roger McPhail)

cent of adder populations were declining and if these trends continued, adders could soon be restricted to just a handful of sites in Britain.

In conclusion Dr Gardner said:

> Our analysis shows that 90% of the sites surveyed have small populations and on average these small populations are declining. When surveyors visit these sites, they typically record less than 10 adders. Only 10% of sites have large populations, which seem to be doing ok. If these trends continue, within 10-20 years, adders will be restricted to just a few sites in the UK, significantly increasing the extinction risk for this priority species in Britain.

The fact that many remaining sites had ten or fewer adult snakes left made them particularly vulnerable to predation or some catastrophic event such as the destruction of their hibernacula. Dr Gardner concluded, 'Our study has shown just how vulnerable our UK adder populations are. And how important it is that we act now to help conserve our adders, before it is too late.'

An adder feeding on a mouse. In Britain there are only a handful of historical records of fatalities due to adder bites and no records of anyone having died in over forty years. (Roger McPhail)

THE DECLINE OF THE ADDER

BOX 3: THE ADDER AND MEDUSA

In Greek mythology, venomous snakes most famously featured in the hair of the three Gorgon sisters whose faces were so hideous that they could turn people to stone just by looking at them. The sisters, Stheno, Euryale and Medusa, were the subject of some of the earliest Greek religious texts written by Homer dating back to 1194-1184 BC. Of the three Gorgon sisters, only Medusa was mortal, using human form to seduce her many victims before eventually being slain by Perseus who cut off her head by looking at her image in the reflection of his bronze shield (from her decapitated head her two children Chrysaor and Pegasus emerged from her union with Poseidon, the Olympian god of the sea).

The most famous depiction of the Greek legend is in the 1618 painting *The Head of Medusa* by the Flemish painter Peter Paul Rubens. It shows her severed head on a table with a mass of harmless grass snakes emerging from it rather than venomous adders. Rubens collaborated on the painting with the famed animal painter Frans Snyders who painted many of the animals in his works. Why didn't Snyders paint venomous adders emerging from her head instead of harmless grass snakes? Both species were then widespread in Belgium and the Netherlands, Snyders depicting the adder in another painting called *Porcupines and Vipers*. Snyders may have liked the colours of grass snakes more or simply thought they would suit the painting better. Or perhaps Rubens asked him not to portray the adder in a gory painting which he knew would shock civilised Flemish society, believing it would simply be too traumatic.

Medusa was transported to the twentieth century in the 1964 Hammer classic *The Gorgon* where she takes human form played by the actress and ballerina Barbara Shelley. Shielded by an infatuated Dr Namaroff played by Peter Cushing, in the final climatic scene she is beheaded by Professor Karl Meister played by Christopher Lee. Shelley was then Hammer's leading lady and was transformed to play Medusa through the use of red eyes and green wrinkly makeup and a rather bizarre wig

The Head of Medusa *by the Flemish painter Peter Paul Rubens was painted in 1618 and showed her severed head on a table with a mass of snakes emerging from it. However, they were not venomous adders but harmless grass snakes. (Rubens)*

THE SECRET LIFE OF THE ADDER

with rubber vipers protruding from it. Although the snakes are clearly vipers, they are green and not very life like, resembling the stylized green pit vipers so beloved of children's toy makers. More recently the story was the basis for the 1981 film *Clash of the Titans* which culminates in Perseus played by Harry Hamlin killing Medusa in the Gorgon's lair. *Clash of the Titans* was notable for being the last film of Ray Harryhausen, who pioneered the stop motion model animation known as Dynamation which was used to bring Medusa to life, although the snakes are again stylized red rubber ones. The film was remade in 2010 with the Russian model Natalia Vodianova playing the role of Medusa and this time the snakes were much more life-like. However, being an Australian-American production they were modelled on the eastern brown snake *Pseudonaja textilis*, a common and highly venomous species in Australia which is responsible for more deaths there than any other species.

Barbara Shelley in the 1964 Hammer classic The Gorgon *playing Medusa. (Colombia Pictures)*

CHAPTER 3

The Ecology of the Adder

Thou shalt tread upon the lion and adder......

Psalms 91:13

The adder, or *Vipera berus* to give the species its full Latin name, is Britain's only venomous snake, a fact which gives it a unique place among our wildlife. It also known by herpetologists or reptile experts by a variety of other names including the viper, the European viper and the northern viper. The adder is one of the most studied reptiles in the world, research having revealed much of its secret life in terms of its biology, ecology and habitat requirements.

Over the last 150 years, many books and a plethora of research papers have been published on the species (seminal historical works are listed in the bibliography).

The adder is one of the most studied reptiles in the world, research having revealed much of its secret life. (Author)

Since the 1970s, there have been many research projects looking at the adder, much pioneering work having recently been done using radio telemetry and genetic studies. Despite this large body of work, much still remains to be found out about the conservation of the adder and in particular its response to climate change, habitat fragmentation, inbreeding and the impact of predators like pheasants.

Distribution and range

The adder belongs to the most sophisticated and evolutionarily advanced family of snakes, the vipers. It is also has the accolade of being the most successful snake in the world, having the largest range and occurring further north than any other species, adders having being recorded at 68° N in Fennoscandia inside the Arctic Circle. To survive this far north, they have evolved several adaptations allowing them to very efficiently absorb any heat from the fleeting Arctic summer. Despite being cold blooded or an ectotherm (their body temperature being dependent on the temperature of their surroundings) this has enabled adders to survive in habitats where other snakes could not live.

These adaptations include their coloration, individuals living further north being much darker so allowing them to absorb more heat than those in the south of their range. They can also fully flatten out their bodies to maximise the surface area exposed to the sun and their skins have special keeled scales which reduce reflection, again helping to absorb more heat. The snake's organs are also greatly elongated, the

A female adder basks in the sun. Despite the adder being extensively studied, climate change, habitat fragmentation, inbreeding and the impact of predators like pheasants need urgent research. (Nick Dobbs)

alimentary canal occupying a third of its body and stretching so it can ingest prey items far larger than itself, allowing the snake to go for long periods without feeding. Finally, snakes living in the far north have also evolved to hibernate longer during the winter months ensuring they only come out when conditions are favourable. These adaptations have allowed the adder to inhabit altitudes of up to 2600m above sea level and to occur above the Arctic Circle, where they have been observed moving across snow.

The adder or viper belongs to a family of snakes called the *Viperidae* which is composed of 13 genera which occur in Europe, Africa and Asia. All the species belonging to the genus *Vipera*, including the adder, are viviparous or produce live young. This gives the genus its Latin name – *vivus* meaning alive and *pario* meaning to bear or bring forth. Of the 21 species in the genus, eight to ten occur in Europe including the two closest relatives of the adder – the aspic adder *Vipera aspis* found in southwest Europe and the meadow viper *Vipera ursinii*, a very rare species found in France, Italy and Greece. They both closely resemble the adder in colour and appearance and have been recorded as interbreeding with them.

Within Britain, the adder is locally distributed from the south coast of England through Wales to the far north of Scotland but is mostly confined to the mainland. In Scotland it occurs on the Inner Herbrides and Arran and in England and

Male adders size each other up. Britain is at the western extremity of the adder's range. (Roger McPhail)

Wales is only found on a few of the closest islands such as Bardsey and the Isle of Wight. It is also famously absent from the island of Ireland. On the continent, the adder occurs across Europe from Britain, the most westerly point in its range, to Mongolia and northern China, a distance of nearly 5,000 miles. Latitudinally, it occurs from the southern tip of Greece as far north as the Arctic Circle, a distance of over 2,000 miles. This distribution gives it the largest range of any snake in the world. Despite being so widespread, there is now increasing evidence that the adder is in decline throughout much of northern Europe, particularly on the edge of its range.

The adder, grass and smooth snakes

The adder is one of three snakes occurring in Britain but can be easily distinguished by its size, behaviour and coloration, in particular the zigzag marking on its back. The others two species, which are both non-venomous, are the grass snake *Natrix helvetica* and the smooth snake *Coronella austriaca*. The most widespread snake in southern England, the Midlands and Wales, the grass or ringed snake is also the longest British snake, growing up to 1.2 metres or four feet in length. Its most distinctive feature is its khaki olive green body and the yellow collar which extends around its neck and the edge of its head. The grass snake has small dark bars along its sides and its underside is pale green with black barring. It is absent from much of Scotland and northern England and in the areas where it overlaps with the adder, its green coloration is

The most widespread snake in southern England, the Midlands and Wales, the grass snake is also the longest British snake, growing up to 1.2 metres or four feet in length. (Pixabay)

usually sufficient to differentiate it. The grass snake can occur in similar habitats to the adder but is much more aquatic and is the snake most likely to be encountered in wetland and riparian habitats like ponds and streams. Due to the decline of the adder, particularly across the Midlands and large parts of southern England, many new sightings of adders often turn out to be grass snakes.

The other species of snake to occur in Britain is the smooth snake which is confined to heathland in Dorset, Hampshire, Surrey and Sussex. A similar shape to the grass snake, it is grey or dull brown in colour with black markings arranged in bars or two rows of dots along its back. Instead of the grass snake's yellow collar, it has a crown pattern on its head. The smooth snake gets its name from its scales which are flat and even, unlike the adder and the grass snake whose scales have a ridge or keel down the middle. It is Britain's rarest reptile and also the most secretive of the three species, which, together with its restricted range and coloration, means it is unlikely to be confused with the adder. The only other widespread 'snake like' species to occur in Britain is the slow worm *Anguis fragilis* which is in fact a legless lizard. Like the adder and grass snake, it is found in a variety of habitats but tends to prefer living underground where it feeds on slugs. Completely harmless, slow worms often appear bronze-like in sunlight, males being paler, sometimes with blue spots, while females have dark sides and a line running down their back. Slow worms only grow to about 50cm in length, have no neck and together with their wormlike appearance mean they are unlikely to be misidentified as an adder.

Above left: The other species of snake to occur in Britain is the smooth snake which is confined to heathland in Dorset, Hampshire, Surrey and Sussex. (Koskoci)

Above right: The only other widespread 'snake like' species to occur in Britain is the slow worm which is in fact a legless lizard. (Author)

The adder is a stocky snake; in Britain, a fully grown adult male can grow up to 60cm or two feet long, the female being a few centimetres longer, with records up to 65cm. The longest that adders are known to reach is in the very north of their range, female adders measuring 85cm having been recorded in Sweden. The tails also distinguish the sexes, the tail of a fully grown male adder being about 7.5 cm or 3 inches long, the females about 6.5cm or two and a half inches long. The male's tail is also thicker as it contains the sex organs and comes to a sharper point, the females being stubbier and less pointed.

The adder is a stocky snake, in Britain a fully grown adult male can grow up to 60cm or two feet long, the female being a few centimetres longer, with records up to 65cm. (Roger McPhail)

THE ECOLOGY OF THE ADDER

BOX 4: WHERE DID THE ADDER GET ITS NAME?

The Saxon poem *Nine Herbs Charm* uses the Old English name for the adder, which was *naeddran* or *naeddre* meaning nether or lower, a reference to it crawling on the ground. Over time, with the development of the English language during the Middle Ages, this became 'nadder' and then 'a nadder' and eventually 'an adder'. Similarly in Gaelic and Old Irish the adder was known as *nathair*, *nathrach* or *nathraichen*. The other title given to the adder is the European viper, the word viper coming from *vipere* in Old Middle English which originated from Latin. *Vipera* is composed of two Latin words: *vivus* meaning 'alive' and *parere* meaning 'to give birth', reflecting the fact that adders give birth to live young.

In Welsh, the adder or viper was known *neidr* and before that the *gwiber*, Welsh legend stating it was a 'flying snake' which lived in its own valley and preyed upon the local community. One day a fearless young man, called Owen ap Gruffydd, vowed to kill the *gwiber* but it ambushed him and after being bitten he fell to his death. The next day his body was found by his friends who in turn ambushed the snake and revenged his death. So to this day the valley near Penmachno in central Wales where the snake was slain is called Wibernant or the valley of the *gwiber*. A very similar legend grew up in Scotland where the large snake-like creature was known as *bethir* (serpent) or *bethir-nimhi* (venomous serpent) in Gaelic.

The adder's name was derived from the Old English naeddran *or* naeddre *meaning nether or lower, a reference to it crawling on the ground. (Roger McPhail)*

56 THE SECRET LIFE OF THE ADDER

Basking and sloughing

Like other reptiles adders cannot generate their own body heat, snakes needing to raise their body temperature to 25°C to 30°C before they can become fully active. So in the spring, adders will bask for long periods on sunny days to increase their body temperature and this is the best time to observe them. Male adders emerge first in late February or early March and bask to mature their sperm, their testes getting much larger with the start of the breeding season.

As the adder grows it sloughs its skin, a process known as ecdysis, which begins after they first emerge from hibernation. Males slough their skin in early April, followed by a subsequent slough at the end of May or the beginning of June. Female adders appear two to three weeks after the males and slough for the first time at the end of May. Both sexes then slough again several times between July and September. On average an adult adder will slough four times a year, but young snakes will moult more often as they grow.

The first sign that an adder is about to slough its skin is that its eye turns milky or cloudy as the old skin begins to break away from the transparent covering of the eye called the brille. This is caused by the secretion of a lubricant beneath the dead skin, during which time the adder cannot see clearly and may hide away until its sight returns. The skin over the head then begins to crack slowly over the period of about a week before the eye becomes clear again. The adder facilitates this by rubbing its

Like other reptiles, the adder cannot generate its own body heat. As a result, they need to bask before they can become fully active. (Roger McPhail)

THE ECOLOGY OF THE ADDER

head over rough ground helping to peel the skin away. Once the head is free the adder will then begin in earnest to shed the remainder of its skin, a process which usually only takes half an hour. Seeking out thick matted grass, bracken or brambles near its hibernation site, the adder will squeeze and push its body through the tangle of vegetation, the friction helping to rub off its old skin, which is discarded inside out, sometimes in one piece.

As the adder grows, it sloughs its skin, a process known as ecdysis, which begins after they first emerge from hibernation. (Roger McPhail)

The presence of old skins woven into the grass or pieces snared on the thorns of brambles is a good indication that snakes are present. Once it has sloughed for the first time in the spring, the adder's colours are then at their brightest, the new skin helping to attract a mate and signifying that the snake is at its peak. The naturalists Brett Westwood and Stephen Moss beautifully described the results in their book *Wonderland* '…the entire translucent skin peels off like a debutante's evening glove, complete with the watch-glass that protects the eye. The males are at their finest now, either golden brown with a darker dorsal zigzag or silvery grey with a blackish zigzag stripe.'

The first sign that an adder is about to slough its skin is that its eye turns milky or cloudy as the old skin begins to break away from the transparent covering of the eye called the brille. (Roger McPhail)

Habitat

The adder is found in a diverse range of habitats in Britain, its former widespread distribution reflecting its adaptability as a species and the abundance of its prey – primarily frogs, lizards and small mammals. In the south of Britain, adders are often associated with dry sandy heaths, commons, meadows, rough grassland, woodland edge and rides (both deciduous and pine), old quarries and on the coast sand dunes and rocky grasslands. However, they can also be found on wetlands, especially around the edges of bogs, along valleys and linear features like hedges, dry stone walls and railway cuttings, particularly disused ones where they like to bask on the old tracks.

Adders can also occasionally turn up in more unusual places, such as airfields, firing ranges, golf courses, gardens or the edge of roads and tracks, normally when they are moving to their summer feeding grounds. In the north of its range, the adder is more closely associated with heather moorlands, coasts and the edge of woods especially in Scotland where it is the only snake to occur. Adders can also be found inside forestry plantations but will disappear once the habitat becomes too overgrown, the same being true of snakes on heaths, commons, meadows and moors. Adders will not usually cross tarmac roads[17] and extensive areas of short mown or heavily grazed grass, these features often acting as barriers to their dispersal.

Adders have complex habitat requirements requiring vegetation and topography that provides for safe hibernacula, basking, mating and feeding areas with corridors that allow safe movement between these locations. The herpetologist Nigel Hand radio tracked 75 adders between April and June and found that males passed through a range of habitats while looking for mates including mature deciduous woodland in early spring before the canopy closed. Ride edges and rough grass were used as corridors, snakes also crossing 'unmade' roads and open mown areas. However, he found adders would not cross heavily grazed or short grassland and tarmac roads, although other observers have recorded them doing this. The male adders in Hand's study moved over 500 metres while searching for mates although one travelled nearly four times this distance. In contrast, females remained within a much smaller area, typically near the hibernacula where they sheltered beneath a gorse bush, bracken mat or bramble patch.

After breeding from early May, both sexes spend protracted periods underground exhibiting fossorial behaviour, when they make extensive use of rodent burrows such as vole runs or spend long periods under vegetation. As a result, they are particularly reliant on plants like gorse, bracken, heather, bramble and on the coast marram grass for cover. Males, non-breeding females and juveniles typically shelter underground for much of the season, only gravid females venturing above ground to bask to help develop the young. Staying underground is important for foraging, protection from predators, escaping inclement weather and as an overnight refuge. So after they have basked in the spring, it is often difficult to find adders in the field during the summer and early autumn as much of their time is spent beneath vegetation.

An adder swallowing a frog with just its legs to go. The adder is found in a diverse range of habitats in Britain from heaths to sand dunes and woods to wetlands. (Roger McPhail)

Above: *An adder emerges from underground to consume a frog. Adders spend long periods beneath vegetation particularly after mating. (Roger McPhail)*

Left: *An adder eats a frog. Adders have complex habitat requirements requiring safe hibernacula, basking areas and feeding grounds with corridors connecting each. (Roger McPhail)*

BOX 5: MYTHS SURROUNDING ADDERS

Over the centuries many myths have grown up about adders. They include:

Female adders swallow their young to protect them – animals taking young inside their mouths for development or protection is rare in nature. Mouthbrooding is behaviour exhibited in some fish such as cichlids, sea catfish and cardinalfish where usually the female but sometimes both parents take the eggs (and more rarely juveniles) inside their mouths. Mouthbrooding is also exhibited in two frogs, the Darwin's and Chile Darwin's frogs, where the young undergo their development in the parents' mouths (although the Chile Darwin's frog is now thought to be extinct). However, it is behaviour that has never been recorded in any snake.

Despite this, the myth was perpetuated for hundreds of years by amateur naturalists and even scientific herpetologists, to the extent that Leighton in his book on British serpents published in 1901 felt the need to dedicate eleven pages to the issue. He wrote:

The next question for consideration is that bone of contention in adder politics – namely, whether the adder-mother does or does not swallow her family....it is astonishing what bitter disputes arise over the discussions of this matter; and I have heard two people holding opposite views on the righteousness of the Boer war argue that question politely, when on the conversation turning to the swallowing theory they become violently abusive and in a very few minutes were hardly on speaking terms.

Leighton wrote about the merits on both sides before concluding with a challenge to the believers, stating 'Let the first person who sees the adder-mother swallow her young proceed to carry out the following programme:-

Secure the mother alive or dead, and tie a ligature securely round the neck.

Take the specimen to any well-known naturalist, and make a statement in the presence of witnesses as to the circumstances attending the capture.

Request the naturalist to dissect the adder in the presence of three reputable witnesses.'

Despite no one successfully completing the challenge, the myth carried on until the outset of the Second World War after which little more was heard or written about it. The myth probably originated when a gravid female adder was killed and found to have well developed young inside her. After giving birth female adders, far from protecting the young in their mouth, have little or no mothering instinct and the young are left to fend for themselves.

Snakes hypnotise their prey – this myth arose because the adder like all other snakes has an unblinking stare. In the Middle Ages, it was believed they hypnotised their prey, immobilizing them long enough to bite. It was a myth most famously repeated in Rudyard Kipling's *Jungle Book* published in 1894 where the python Kaa hypnoties Mowgli telling him 'Look me in the eye when I'm speaking to you.' The reality is that snakes have no eyelids so cannot close their eyes or blink. Instead, they have a thin, clear membrane covering their corneas, called appropriately enough spectacles or brilles. Although they cannot close their eyes, they can close their retinas when sleeping.

Adders don't die until dusk – adders are tough animals who can sometimes survive violent attacks by foxes, crows or even people. As a result, a superstition

One of the adder's most prominent features is their red eyes and vertical slit pupils which over the centuries have perpetuated their 'demonic', image. (Nick Dobbs)

> grew up that mortally wounded snakes will not die until dusk. Legend had it that the only way to kill a snake was to cut off its head and then wait until after sunset to ensure that it was dead. The myth probably arose because after death a snake's body can sometimes continue to move. These writhing movements are not because the snake is still alive but are short-lived reflexes and spasms.
>
> *It's bad luck to cross the path of an adder* – ancient Britons believed that crossing the path of an adder would bring misfortune, seeing one on the way to market meaning that you would not sell your goods that day. Dreaming about adders was also a bad omen as it meant that your enemies were plotting against you. In Dorset, an adder on your doorstep meant someone in the house was going to die. In the Welsh version, a male and a female snake appearing near the house signalled the death of the owner. To keep adders away, wormwood, an aromatic herb, was planted outside the house and lily roots, ash tree boughs, hartshorn (ground up deer antlers), and even old shoes were burnt outside to produce a pungent odour. Like all myths it contains a modicum of truth as adders are known to dislike smoke, associating it with fire.

Markings

The adder is a beautiful snake, especially after it has just shed its skin in the spring and its colours are at their most vivid. Adders are unusual among snakes in that they exhibit great diversity and sexual dimorphism in their coloration. Males are generally brighter coloured than females, their base coloration ranging from ochre to deep brown, but their most usual colour is cream or silvery grey. Females are normally a duller reddish brown or yellow-brown. Both sexes have the distinctive black zigzag pattern or diamond stripe along their backs which is their most characteristic feature, the first diamond often being quite variable, the pattern then becoming more regular.

Research has shown that many would-be predators recognize the adder's classic zigzag markings as a sign that the species is venomous and avoid the snakes, a defence mechanism known as aposematism.[18] Their coloration also provides superb cryptic camouflage, helping to break up the adder's outline and blend in with their surroundings. Female adders in particular are almost indistinguishable from the russet hues of bracken in the autumn when they most need to 'disappear' as they prepare to give birth.

In common with their base coloration, the zigzag marking can also vary in some snakes from 'wavy blotches' to an almost straight black line although this is very rare.

A newly sloughed male adder in the spring. Males are generally brighter coloured than females, their base coloration ranging from ochre to deep brown, but their most usual colour is cream or silvery grey. (Roger McPhail)

Females are normally a duller reddish brown or yellow-brown. (Ray Hamilton)

THE SECRET LIFE OF THE ADDER

The adder's classic zigzag pattern on their backs mark them out as being venomous, shown clearly here on a male adder. (Author)

THE ECOLOGY OF THE ADDER

The herpetologist Gerald Leighton in his book on British serpents described an adder with these markings:

> The late Mr Kirby of Ulverston once met with [a] very remarkable viper .... He showed it to me a short time before his death. It was taken with his own hands in the neighbourhood of Ulverston, where he lived for so long. It was unique in his experience. The ground colour of this snake is uniformly olive-grey. The curious feature is that the usual zigzag dorsal pattern is entirely absent, and has been replaced by [an] even ribbon-like black band.

Other defining characteristics, most easily spotted when adders are basking out in the open in spring, are that both sexes have a series of scales or platelets on their head and an X or inverted V shape marking on the back of their neck. These marks can vary greatly, Leighton noting that they were slightly different in each snake, more recent research carried out by the herpetologist Sylvia Sheldon proving that the head pattern is unique and can be used to identify individuals (see Box 9). Apart from its markings, one of the adder's most prominent features is their red eyes with vertical slit pupils which over the centuries have perpetuated their 'demonic' image. Far from having an 'evil eye', adders in common with all other snakes have no eyelids so cannot

In common with their base coloration, the zigzag marking can also vary in some snakes from 'wavy blotches' to an almost straight black line although this is rare. (Roger McPhail)

The most striking colour variant is the black or melanistic adder which gave the television comedy series Blackadder *its name. (Ray Hamilton)*

blink. As a result, they are always very protective of their eyes, in bright sunshine ensuring that their pupils are in shade to prevent them from being damaged.

Juvenile adders are a different colour from their parents, being orange-brown or more reddish, coloration which helps them blend in with the bracken but is lost as they mature. This colour variation gave rise to the belief that 'small red adders' were a separate species, a myth championed by Leighton and many other amateur herpetologists right up to the Second World War. However, the most striking colour variant is the black or melanistic adder which gave the television comedy series Blackadder its name. In some parts of Britain, black adders are relatively common although they are very rarely completely black. In contrast albino adders are extremely scarce and don't survive long in the wild due to their lack of camouflage.

Fangs

Over time snakes have evolved three types of teeth – solid or recurved teeth found in many species including the grass snake and smooth snake, grooved teeth found in back-fanged or semi-venomous snakes and the tubular fangs found in venomous

THE ECOLOGY OF THE ADDER

species like the adder. The adder's venom-conducting fangs are the most evolved of all snake teeth, being hinged at the base so that they can be folded back along the roof of the mouth when they are not being used. This allows the snake to have much longer fangs than it could otherwise accommodate in its jaw, enabling them to inject venom deeper into their prey.

The jaw on the adder, like that of the grass snake, can be unhinged enabling it to eat much larger prey items than it could otherwise swallow. The fangs on an adder typically measure 4-7mm in length and are curved backward towards the throat and end in a very fine point. Each can be operated independently, giving the snake maximum flexibility when it comes to immobilising its quarry. When the adder is about to strike, the lower jaw is opened, the upper jaw is unhinged and the fangs are brought forward ready to bite.

Tubular in structure, the fangs work like a hypodermic needle with a small hole just above the tip through which the venom is driven when the snake bites. The venom is produced and stored in modified salivary glands situated just below the eyes, a special duct supplying the fangs. The fangs are protected by a sheath composed of a pocket of skin, at the back of which are an array of replacements fangs in case the ones in use break or get damaged. A total of three or four reserve teeth are lined up, the next tooth being in position before the old one is shed.

When basking, adders will sometimes 'yawn', opening their mouths as wide as possible. During this procedure, the adder realigns both its fangs and its jaw, each fang being raised and lowered individually while the jaw is moved from side to side. This particularly happens after the adder has bitten its prey and swallowed it. Fangs are also naturally shed over time and replaced with new ones to ensure that they are always in perfect working order.

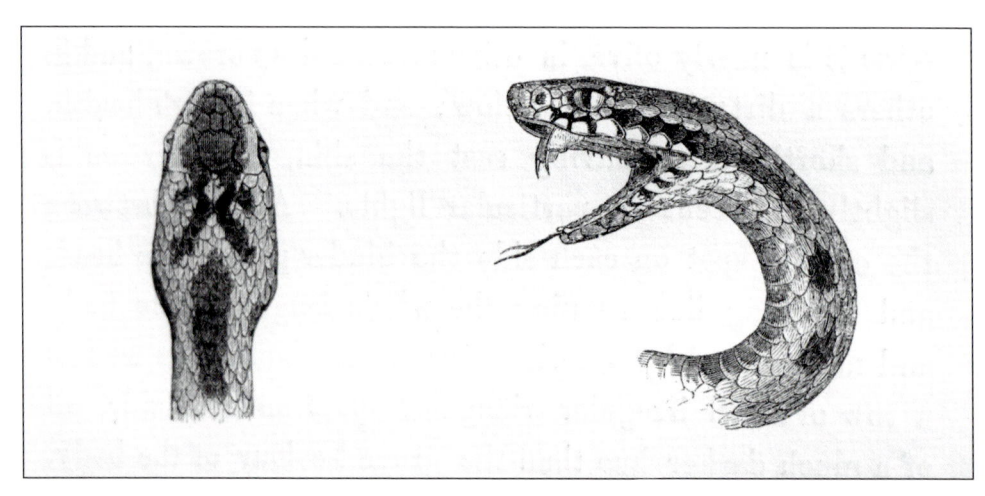

Head and side profile of an adder from Thomas Bell's 1846 book on British reptiles. The adder's venom-conducting fangs are the most evolved of all snake teeth and can be folded back along the roof of the mouth. (J.V. Voorst)

THE VIPER, OR ADDER.

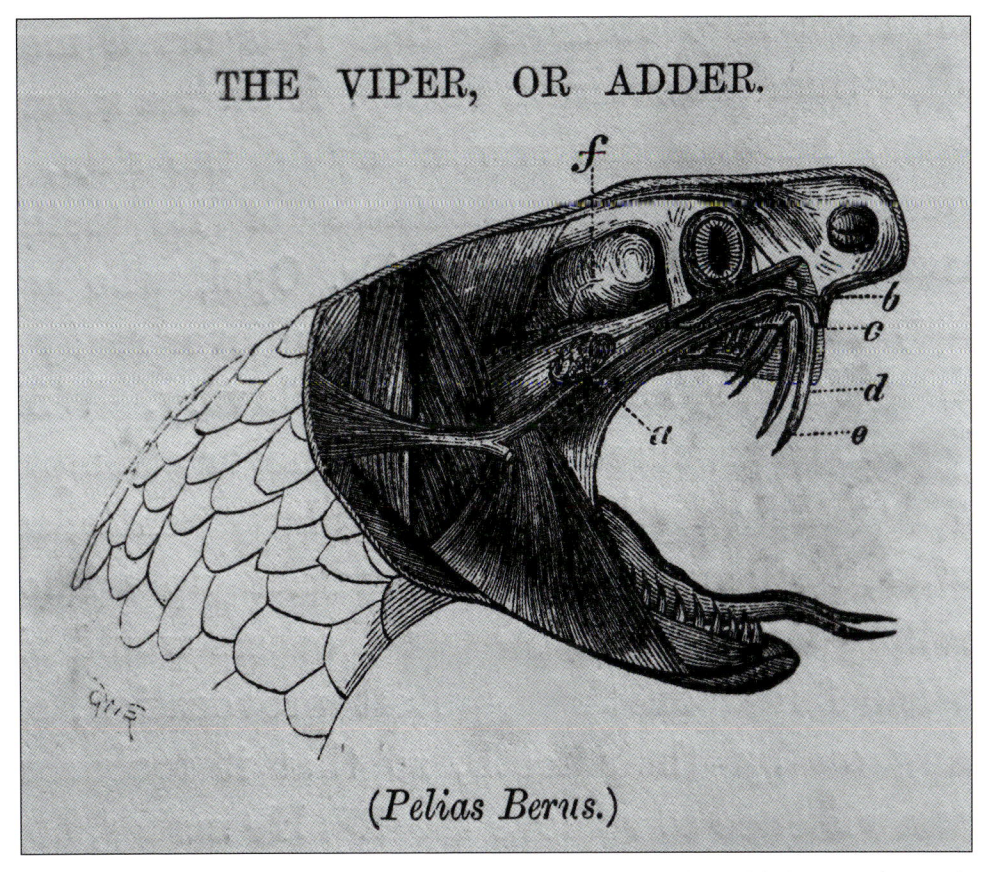

(Pelias Berus.)

The adder's fangs from the first pocket book on British reptiles by M.C. Cooke published in 1865 showing the replacement fangs stored in the roof of the mouth. Key a – venom producing gland, b duct, c base of fang d curved tube, e opening or slit f nerve. (R. Hardwicke)

Venom

The venom of the adder is generally of little danger to people and while an adder bite can be very painful and cause a nasty inflammation, it is really only dangerous to the very young, ill or elderly. Produced by modified salivary glands, the venom is injected 2-3 mm under the skin of the prey or if they are unlucky enough to be bitten, a person's skin. It is a yellow liquid and contains a complex mixture of proteins and peptides, enzymes which break down molecules in the body, targeting the blood, cells and tissues. The venom works by being toxic to living cells and causing internal bleeding and is classified by toxicologists as being cytotoxic and haemorrhagic.

According to the Amphibian and Reptile Conservation Trust (ARC) the symptoms after being bitten include shock; severe pain at the location of the bite; swelling, redness and bruising; nausea and vomiting; diarrhoea; itchy lumps on the skin;

swelling of the lips, tongue, gums and throat; breathing difficulties; mental confusion, dizziness or fainting and irregular heartbeat.

Not all of these symptoms will be seen in all cases, and the severity of them will vary greatly depending on the amount of venom injected. The ARC calculates that in around 70 per cent of cases there will be no or very little poisoning or envenomation, leading to only local symptoms such as pain and swelling. In addition, the adder can deliver a dry bite in which no venom is injected, this accounting for a third of bites to humans and acts as a warning signal. In rare cases there can be a range of more serious effects including kidney failure, anaphylaxis, heavy blood loss, coma and cardiac arrest. When symptoms are severe it is vital to administer an anti-venom together with an injection of adrenaline to counter the effects of anaphylactic shock.

The most comprehensive review of the effect of adder bites was carried out by H. Alistair Reid, a consultant physician and senior lecturer at the Liverpool School of Tropical Medicine. It was published in 1976 in the *British Medical Journal*, a year after the last recorded fatality in Britain. He reviewed 95 cases of adder bite that had occurred in Britain over the previous 100 years and concluded 'Most bites occurred in men who foolishly picked up the adder.'[19] Reid also reported that three-quarters of the victims reached a hospital within two hours of the bite, noting that children recovered quickly but adults may 'take weeks or months to recover during which there may be considerable disability in the bitten limb'. The early symptoms

The adder's venom is produced by modified salivary glands and is designed to overcome its prey like this frog. (Roger McPhail)

The adders venom is toxic but there have been no fatalities in over 40 years. A medical review of adder bites concluded 'Most bites occurred in men who foolishly picked up the adder.' (Roger McPhail)

included 'local swelling and discolouration, vomiting, diarrhoea and early collapse, which often resolves spontaneously. In severe poisoning, persistent or recurrent shock is the main feature.'

Reid reported that deaths were very rare, only 14 being recorded in the previous 100 years and numbers were much smaller than fatalities from bee and wasp stings, writing, 'In England and Wales only one death from adder bite was recorded from 1950-72, but there were 61 deaths from bee or wasp stings.' In terms of treatment, he concluded, 'In most cases simple symptomatic treatment is enough, but all patients should be carefully monitored. With persistent or recurrent shock Zagreb antivenom is indicated; and it should also be considered in adults seen within two hours of the bite to minimise morbidity from local effects.' Since Reid wrote his paper, there have been no deaths from adder bites but there are two to nine deaths a year due to anaphylaxis from bee or wasp stings.

Senses

The adder is equipped with a range of complex sense organs for catching its prey, finding a mate and escaping from predators who may eat it. Adders have no ear drum so many people assume them to be deaf. However, while they have no external ear or eardrum, they can still detect sound, their lower jawbone being highly sensitive to low frequency vibrations that travel through the ground. This is the reason that all many people see of an adder is their tail as they slither away, their footsteps alerting the snake to their presence. The vibrations are detected by tiny bones in the lower jaw and then transmitted to the 'inner ear' in the skull via a delicate bony rod called the quadrate bone. Adder jaw bones can move up, down, left and right independently so as they crawl on the ground, they can detect the location or direction of a sound, such as footsteps, through their jaw.

The adder with its head on the ground is therefore in a very good position to detect any sounds conducted through the earth. However, recent research has shown that snakes are able to detect both airborne and ground borne vibrations using their body surface, known as somatic hearing.[20] Some herpetologists also believe they can detect some airborne noises using their lung, which as well as breathing may help amplify sound. In the adder only the right lung remains, the left one being vestigial, the front part instead acting as reservoir through which sound may be conducted.

In contrast to their hearing, an adder's eyesight is well developed although by human standards they can appear short sighted, the eyes responding mainly to movement rather than creating a composite picture. The adder has no eyelids, instead the eye being protected by the brille, a transparent membrane, which allows limited movement. It is believed that adders can see contrasting colours and shapes but not

The adder can detect vibrations through its jawbone so it is often long gone before people come across it. (Author)

in detail. The retina of the adder's eye is rich in rods, which means that the animal is able to see well in the dark but also contains cones allowing it daylight vision. The adder's eyes are therefore very sensitive to light, which is the reason it has an elliptic pupil, an adaptation to protect the adder's eyes from strong light.

The most acutely developed sense in the adder is that of smell and like all snakes they 'taste' the air with their tongues. The forked tongue is regularly flicked in and out, picking up scent particles which the adder uses to find its prey and also to navigate its way around. After biting its prey or when frightened, the tongue is flicked in and out constantly as the snake seeks to gather as much information as possible about its intended target or its environment. Once detected, scent particles are transferred to a special olfactory structure called the Jacobson's organ which is situated in an aperture in the roof of the mouth. The adder uses this organ to follow its stricken prey as its venom incapacitates it. The tongue is also used as a tactile organ, the snake using it to find out about dead prey or other potential prey items and is used in reproduction, the male flicking his tongue over the female to 'taste' her prior to mating.

Adders can also hiss if they feel threatened, the sound coming from air passing through the snake's mouth. Snakes breathe through an organ in their throat just behind the tongue called the glottis. During normal breathing, the glottis opens and closes into the trachea or windpipe. However, an adder can forcibly expel air from the glottis making a small piece of cartilage inside vibrate, making the hissing sound. When consuming large prey, the glottis can be extended out to the side of the adder's mouth allowing it to breathe as it swallows.

The most acutely developed sense in the adder is that of smell and like all snakes they 'taste' the air with their tongues. (Roger McPhail)

BOX 6: A NEW SNAKE SPECIES FOR BRITAIN?

In Gerald Leighton's 1901 book on snakes, he championed the controversial theory that there were two adder species in Britain – the common adder and the 'small red viper'. Leighton's hypothesis was disproved but over a century later a new species of snake was announced. In 2017, there was a lot of media coverage about a new species of grass snake being discovered in Britain emanating from research carried out by the Senckenberg Research Institute in Germany. They published the results of a study into the genetics of more than 1,600 grass snakes across Europe which found that there were two different subspecies present – the western grass snake *Natrix natrix helvetica* which is native to Britain and the eastern grass snake *Natrix natrix natrix* which occurs in Eastern Europe and is only present in Britain in small numbers as a result of introductions. Across their European range, the scientists found there was only a narrow contact zone between the two sub species with little genetic mixing and so they taxonomically split them into separate species. As a result, the British grass snake is now known as the western barred grass snake *Natrix helvetica*, when it was previously classified as *Natrix natrix*, the reclassification mistakenly being reported as a new snake species for Britain in much of the media.

In 1901, the herpetologist Gerald Leighton hoped to prove the existence of a new adder species but failed. In 2017 the grass snake was split into two separate subspecies. (Author)

Movement

Adders are adept at disappearing long before many people see or come across them, quickly moving into cover or going underground to escape unwanted attention. However, there are times when adders are much more visible, and it is possible to get a better view of them. These are in early spring when they are basking to increase their body temperature, when males are searching for mates and when adders are moving to their summer feeding grounds. Adders are generally ground dwelling creatures who move rather slowly but they are capable of fast bursts of speed and can also climb and swim well.

Adders, like many cold-blooded species living in temperate climates, are very efficient at using energy and will only put the minimum amount of effort into movement, relying a lot on their camouflage and venom for protection. If undisturbed the adder usually moves in an unhurried way, using its abdomen muscles to push itself along the ground. Viewed from below through a plate of glass, the powerful muscles pushing the snake along in an undulating series of belly strokes can be clearly seen.

The average speed of an adder while exploring its territory or looking for prey is about 3mph, equivalent to a slow walking pace in people. However, when disturbed or alarmed the adder is capable of very quick bursts of speed, propelling itself along

A male adder moves through the bracken. Adders put the minimum amount of energy into locomotion but are capable of moving very quickly when they need to. (Roger McPhail)

in a series of s-shaped loops, using any undulations on the ground for leverage. In this way the head follows the body in a graceful, almost effortless way, a beautiful form of locomotion best observed when adders are swimming. The adder's abdomen muscles also come into their own when male adders are fighting for dominance in pursuit of a mate, a spectacular event called the dance of the adders.

Hibernation

When adders emerge from hibernation in the spring, their priority is basking to increase their body temperature and – in the case of the males – finding a mate. Hibernation in Britain used to typically last 3-4 months, adders going underground with the shortening days of autumn to escape the cold winter weather. Hibernacula include old rabbit burrows, south facing banks and crevices in the root systems beneath trees. During this period, to conserve energy adders shut down all but their essential body functions, living off their body reserves of fat accumulated during the summer. Adders will hibernate on their own or with other snakes including different species like the grass snake, the animals coiling together in a ball as a way of conserving heat. However, in recent years with a changing climate, adders have not gone into a deep hibernation, instead becoming active on warmer winter days and during a sufficiently long period of milder weather often emerging from hibernation. In 2019, due to our changing climate, it was confirmed for the first time that adders had been seen in every month of the year.[21]

Male adders now emerge from hibernation in late February to early March, typically two to three weeks before the females. However, the date of emergence has been becoming earlier and has fluctuated more, the herpetologist Peter Stafford writing back in 1987 that male adders usually emerged 'towards the end of March' followed by juveniles and females in April.[22] On first coming out, the males will take every opportunity to bask to increase their body temperature and manufacture their sperm supply ready for mating. It is at this time of the year that adders are at their most sluggish and vulnerable, male adders often basking out in the open and flattening their bodies to maximise absorption of the suns heat. When the females emerge, they give off a powerful scent from their anal glands if they are ready for mating which can be detected by male adders hundreds of metres away.

Females usually take up favoured spots not far from the hibernacula and due to the pungency of their scent can attract males from several different sites. A female adder's scent is a powerful odour which is detectable by people, the male seeking her out using his tongue. Female adders in Britain usually only give birth every other year, a slow rate of reproduction which is compensated for by snakes living relatively long lives. The normal life expectancy for an adder is 5-10 years in the wild although

Above: A male adder with a female. Dominant males will often mate with several females. (Roger McPhail)

Below: An adder sloughing its skin. Adders typically live 5-10 years in the wild. (Roger McPhail)

female adders who are 15 years old and more have been recorded. The herpetologist Sylvia Sheldon in her pioneering work in the Wyre Forest followed several individuals for over ten years (see Box 9). This included a mature female first seen in 1983 known as Notches, who Sheldon estimated to be at least eight years old when she was first recorded in 1983 and was last seen in 2004 making her approximately 29 years old.

Mating

If a female adder is in season, she will wave her tail seductively, the male adder tapping her up rapidly with his chin and flicking his tongue in and out all over her body. This ritual may last several hours before copulation takes place when the two snakes can be joined together for up to an hour. A male adder's penis is a bulbous organ called a hemipenis, a paired structure composed of two penes. They are situated at the base of the tail and are cylindrical in shape and hollow to accommodate the spermatic fluid, the hemipenis being turned inside out when aroused. The male's testes are yellowish-white in colour and are situated under the kidneys, in the females the ovaries occupying a similar position.

During mating the male pushes a loop of his body beneath the female to bring his hempenis into contact with her cloaca or vent. The adder's hemipenis is covered in hooks and spikes which are used to hold on to the female as the sperm is being transferred

Mating adders. The male pushes a loop of his body beneath the female so his hempenis comes into contact with her cloaca. (Nick Dobbs)

to her body. The appendages also ensure that the two remain joined together during copulation. Adders can copulate several times in a day, mating typically taking place under deep cover such as bracken. Once released, the male adder will then guard the female for a day or two to stop other adders mating with her.

If a rival male appears during the early or later stages of mating, the courting male will immediately challenge the interloper and give chase. Both snakes then take part in ritualised combat, wrapping their bodies around each other and moving very quickly through the undergrowth at high speed before coming to a sudden halt. Each adder will then try to intimidate his competitor by swaying and weaving in

Two male adders size each other up. If neither backs down, they will fight. (Roger McPhail)

front of him and then placing his jaw on the other's body to test out how strong he is. If neither snake gives way, this culminates in them both intertwining and rising up together in a spectacular trial of strength known as the dance of the adders. The winner is the adder which can force his opponent to the ground, the loser then beating a hasty retreat and bolting for cover.

The adder's abdomen muscles come into their own when male adders are fighting for dominance in pursuit of a mate, a spectacular event called the dance of the adders. (Roger McPhail)

This combat can last up to half an hour during which both snakes are so engrossed in each other that they are often oblivious to predators and even human spectators. Interestingly, despite being venomous, neither adder attempts to bite the other, perhaps sensing that this would be matched by a retaliatory strike which would leave both combatants immobilised or more likely adders are immune to their own venom. After mating, male adders will then go in search of another female, dominant males often copulating with several females during the mating season.

The fight culminates in them both intertwining and rising up together in a trial of strength. (Roger McPhail)

The winner is the one which forces his opponent to the ground. (Roger McPhail)

Young

Female adders can breed at three years old, but most do not give birth until they are eight or more. Giving birth puts a great strain on the adder's body, so very young snakes who do give birth often do not survive the winter. This is also the reason why adders only give birth every other year, females using the next season to put build up their reserves and get into condition. While some snakes can under exceptional circumstances give birth every year, this is now considered rare in Britain. Where their prey is in short supply or female adders are under stress, for example due to inbreeding or disturbance, it can be up to four or five years before they give birth again. The female's gestation period typically lasts for three to four months, the young being born at the end of August or the beginning of September. This means that adders have a low rate of reproduction, a factor compensated for in part by them being long lived.

Female adders give birth to live young which are wrapped in a transparent membrane which raptures when the young snake pushes against it with its head. The number of young can vary greatly, between six and 20 typically being recorded depending on the age and condition of the female. When born, baby adders are

Juvenile adders are a different colour from their parents being orange-brown or more reddish. (Roger McPhail)

approximately 15-20cm long and are exact replicas of their parents although a different colour, the ratio of males to females being roughly equal. Young adders are capable of looking after themselves from birth being equipped with both fangs and a good supply of venom but often stay close to their mother for up to a week. During this time, their priority is to find safety and bask, their internal reserves providing enough food for the first few critical weeks of life. If suddenly alarmed, baby adders can occasionally seek refuge under their mother, behaviour which gave rise to the myth that female adders swallow their young for protection (see Box 5).

Female adders in Britain usually only give birth every other year, meaning they have a slow rate of reproduction. (Roger McPhail)

Neonatal adders and young snakes will hunt for tadpoles, baby newts, new-born lizards and baby mice. Interestingly, young adders will eat tiny frogs whole, saving their venom for more sizeable prey. Young born in September need to feed quickly before going into hibernation, as their next meal will not be until the following spring, meaning they will have to survive over winter on their fat reserves. Despite being venomous, young adders are extremely vulnerable in the first few weeks of life, many providing a bite sized snack for a whole host of predators from foxes to pheasants.

Between six and 20 young are born depending on the age and condition of the female. (Roger McPhail)

Above: *The live young are born at the end of August or the beginning of September. (Roger McPhail)*

Left: *They are wrapped in a transparent membrane which ruptures when the young snake pushes against it with its head. (Roger McPhail)*

Feeding

Adders do not need to eat often, surviving for six or seven months of the year on their reserves of body fat during the winter and spring. Adders are able to do this because they are extremely efficient at using energy and being cold-blooded do not have to expend it maintaining a constant body temperature. However, from early May they start hunting in earnest, adders feeding on a wide variety of prey including frogs, toads, newts, slow worms, mice and voles. Juveniles will also eat insects, spiders and earthworms. Adders are great opportunists, taking whatever prey they come across, but will particularly search out areas with young frogs, lizards and small mammals such as the long-tailed field mouse, wood mouse, bank vole and the short-tailed field vole. They will also climb trees to eat fledgling birds and if sufficiently hungry, an adder will not hesitate to bite any small animal that comes within striking range.

The trigger for any bite is for the adder to detect movement, prey which remains motionless being passed by. On locating their quarry, adders strike in a split second, powerful muscles injecting the venom deep into their victim after which the snake quickly releases it to avoid being injured in the struggle. The stricken prey will then either die or limp away, the adder following its scent trail until it is overcome by the venom, usually within a few minutes. If the animal is still alive, the adder will then wait for it to die before swallowing its prey whole. The snake's jaws detach from the skull so that the adder can fully stretch its mouth over its quarry, this elasticity

An adder has bitten a wood mouse and waits for its venom to take effect. (Roger McPhail)

Above: The adder then eats the mouse headfirst. (Roger McPhail)

Below: After the head, the adder's jaws envelop the whole body. (Roger McPhail)

enabling the snake to eat prey far bigger than it is. The adder then consumes its prey beginning at the head and then enveloping the whole body, after which powerful digestive juices in the snake's gullet begin to dissolve the victim.

A small mammal will always be swallowed headfirst but other prey like a frog is eaten from either end. Small prey items like froglets are ingested quickly in a matter of minutes, the food being moved down the adder's gullet using a powerful muscular wave action which pushes it along aiding digestion. However, if an adder kills a fully grown frog or small mammal, they can take up to half an hour to be consumed and then in the case of the mammal several days to digest the fur, skull and bones. During this time, the distended adder is sluggish, one large meal often lasting it for several weeks. During a typical season, a fully grown adder may consume five to ten frogs, newts and small mammals. Adders also need to drink and will regularly visit streams, ponds and puddles during hot weather, dipping their snout beneath the surface and drawing water in through the opening used by the tongue.

After mating, male and non-breeding female adders will begin the journey from their hibernacula to their summer feeding grounds in search of prey, favouring low lying wet or boggy areas such as water meadows, waterlogged heaths and the edges of sphagnum bogs. These areas are often rich in frogs, a favoured prey item particularly of young snakes. Adders will travel surprisingly long distances in search of good feeding grounds, older male snakes in particular having favoured hunting habitats which can up to a 1.6km or a mile from where they hibernated. The herpetologist Sylvia Sheldon found that in non-breeding years, females can also range over a

The snake's jaws detach from the skull so that the adder can fully stretch its mouth over the mouse. (Roger McPhail)

Above: The elasticity in the jaw enables the adder to eat prey far bigger than it is. (Roger McPhail)

Left: It will take the adder several days to digest the fur, skull and bones. (Roger McPhail)

wide area in pursuit of prey species. A female adder she followed in 2007 moved half a kilometre between two sites and in 1994 another female moved just over one kilometre. This journey can take several days and is often when people out walking come across them. Here they will spend the next four months of their lives before beginning the journey back to their hibernation sites in the early autumn.

Predators

The adder has a wide range of natural predators, of whom probably the most common are birds. Birds of prey like kestrels, kites and buzzards will readily take snakes if they come across them, buzzards often on finding an adder out basking returning to the site to see if can catch any others. All members of the corvid family, including crows, jackdaws, jays, magpies, ravens and rooks, are known to predate adders, especially carrion crows whose numbers have increased dramatically in recent years. Seagulls and herons will also kill and eat adders if they come into contact with them. However, probably the single most prolific predator of adders now at many sites near shoots are game birds, especially pheasants, over sixty million birds being released annually into the British countryside. Mammalian predators will also take their toll, badgers, foxes, hedgehogs, rats, stoats, weasels and pine martens all eating adders. There are also records of adders being recovered from the stomachs of pikes and eels, proof that they are good swimmers and will readily cross ponds and rivers.

Adders are particularly susceptible to predators at the start of the breeding season. In the spring after sloughing male adders are more likely to be killed by aerial predators but in the summer, females are attacked more.[23] After emerging, males are vulnerable because they often bask in the open and following sloughing stand out more. They are especially prone to predation when travelling in search of a mate or between sites.

The adder has a wide range of natural predators, the most common being birds like this kestrel. (Sachin Nihcas)

In contrast, gravid female adders stay much closer to the hibernacula during the spring where their cryptic markings camouflage them well. However, over the passage of a summer, they are more likely to be caught out in the open by predators as they spend longer periods above ground basking to develop the young.

The relationship between adders and predators is a complex one but it is likely that in recent years the numbers of adders killed by predators like carrion crows has increased markedly, especially in comparison to those killed by people or dying a natural death. This is particularly the case where game bird numbers are high which also results in greater local concentrations of native predators including buzzards, crows, magpies, foxes and rats.

Left: All members of the corvid family are known to predate adders, especially carrion crows whose numbers have increased dramatically in recent years. (Pixabay)

Below: The single most prolific predator of adders near shoots are game birds, especially pheasants, over sixty million birds now being released annually into the British countryside. (Nestor Montagu)

Adders are not susceptible to many natural diseases or parasites but potentially the most dangerous one is snake fungal disease (SFD). First recorded in North America, SFD is caused by the fungal pathogen *Ophidiomyces ophiodiicola* and in 2015 it was first detected in a wild grass snake in Britain. Symptoms of the disease include skin lesions, scabs and crusty scales, heavily infected snakes often succumbing to the disease. While it has not been recorded in adders yet, the disease could pose another potential threat to Britain's dwindling adder population.

The law

As well as natural predators and diseases, large numbers of adders are also still killed by people each year despite this being illegal. Adders are fully protected under the 1981 Wildlife and Countryside Act and it is an offence to kill, injure or trade them. They are also classified as a Priority Species in the UK Biodiversity Action Plan and protected by a whole suite of other laws such as site designations and planning policies.

As adders are fully protected by law it means that snakes found on sites scheduled for development have to be moved to alternative habitats. However, translocation of adders is controversial as they are known to be extremely faithful to traditional sites. So translocating adders is often done only as a last resort, research showing that moved snakes have a higher mortality rate reducing the chances of establishing a new population.[24]

Two male adders fighting over a female. Adders are fully protected under the 1981 Wildlife & Countryside Act. (Roger McPhail)

BOX 7: SNAKES IN POPULAR CULTURE

Reflecting their central role in our culture, snakes feature prominently in films, on television and in the popular press. In 2019, the American journalist Chris Nashawaty published 'The 14 Best Snake Moments in Movie History' in *Vulture* magazine. In response to the release of the 2019 thriller *Them That Follow*, which features a mass of writhing, rattling, poisonous snakes, Nashawaty wrote, 'It seemed like as good an excuse as any to tuck our pants into our socks, bust out the anti-venom, and play armchair herpetologist, examining Hollywood's long, hiss-of-death love affair with nature's deadliest reptiles.'

At number 14 in his list, Nashawaty ranked the 1967 film *Jungle Book* with the 'crafty' snake Kaa while at six he chose the giant serpent in the 2002 movie *Harry Potter and the Chamber of Secrets*, a snake 'that instantly kills those who make eye contact with it.' At five he selected the comical 2006 film *Snakes on a Plane*, while the runner up was the celebrated film maker Steven Spielberg's hero Indiana Jones who reveals his phobia of snakes in the 1981 film *Raiders of the Lost Ark*. However, Nashawaty's number one snake movie was the 1997 horror flick *Anaconda* which features a 40-foot snake who swallows people whole before regurgitating them. 'There are many great deaths by snake in cinema, but there can only be one Greatest,' Nashawaty wrote, 'It's pure B-movie bliss.' In none of films are snakes portrayed in a positive light or as being anything other than devious, dangerous or downright evil.

Snakes fair better when it comes to television, starring in many natural history and countryside programmes. A good example was the 2015 series of the BBC programme *Springwatch* where millions of viewers followed the fortunes of radio tracked adders at the RSPB's Minsmere reserve. However, there has still not been a television programme made about conservation of the adder, film makers being very reluctant to make a programme which deals with thorny issues like the impact of game birds or dogs on snakes. *The Wild Isles*, a major landmark series about British natural history, is being produced by the independent natural history company Silverback Films. Silverback was formed in 2012 by Alastair Fothergill and Keith Scholey and is now a very profitable company employing over 100 people who make bluechip natural history programmes for very big clients like Disneynature and BBC Studios. Fothergill, who has worked with David Attenborough over many years, also makes programmes featuring Prince William, someone who actively participates in royal shoots but also champions conservation. Although *The Wild Isles* series features the

A black adder in Thomas Bell's 1846 book on British reptiles. In some parts of Britain, black adders are relatively common although they are rarely completely black. (J. V. Voorst)

adder, Fothergill has stated that it will not include any issues to do with its conservation as these are 'too political'[25].

The melanistic form of the adder also famously featured on the opening credits of the very popular BBC series *Blackadder*. The character of Edmund Blackadder, brilliantly played by Rowan Atkinson, perfectly captured the 'crafty' side of the adder's nature. However, any positive publicity is dwarfed by the slew of sensational stories which are published every year in the popular press about adder bites. Many of these end up on regional television news and magazine programmes, helping to perpetuate the false stereotype that the adder is a dangerous snake only too willing to bite its unwary victims.

The 14 Best Snake Moments in Movie History. By Chris Nashawaty.

14. *The Jungle Book* (1967)
13. *The Snake Woman* (1961)
12. *Piranhaconda* (2012)
11. *Hard Target* (1993)

10. *Clash of the Titans* (1981)
 9. *Venom* (1991)
 8. *Conan the Barbarian* (1982)
 7. *Sssssss* (1973)
 6. *Harry Potter and The Chamber Of Secrets* (2002)
 5. *Snakes on a Plane* (2006)
 4. *Kill Bill 2* (2004)
 3. *King Kong* (1933)
 2. *Raiders of the Lost Ark* (1981)
 1. *Anaconda* (1997)

The 1997 horror flick Anaconda features a 40-foot snake who swallows people whole before regurgitating them. Most films portray snakes as devious, dangerous and evil. (Columbia Pictures)

CHAPTER 4

The Threats to the Adder

......adders' poison is under their lips.

Psalms 140:3

The adder has been declining in Britain since the Second World War but in the last couple of decades the rate has accelerated as populations have become ever smaller and more isolated. The naturalists Brett Westwood and Stephen Moss summed up the adders predicament in their book *Wonderland*:

> They are magnificent animals and one of the genuine sadnesses of recent times is that they have gone for ever from some sites where [we]'ve known them for many years. For ever is an ominous phrase, but in the case of adders it is almost certainly true. Human persecution is part of the problem, as is simplification of

Two male adders investigate each other. The adder is an indicator species of the health of our biodiversity, a barometer of how we treat the natural world. (Nick Dobbs)

habitat: too much shading can force snakes into less suitable areas and, because they hibernate communally, a forestry bulldozer can easily wipe out large elements of the population. In the case of mature females this can be disastrous.

In 2020, the Amphibian and Reptile Groups of the UK held a seminar looking at the threats to adders called 'Meeting the challenges of conserving adders in a 21st Century landscape – lessons from England and France'. The seminar brought together both leading British and French herpetologists who discussed the challenges they faced in conserving adders. Among the many threats they listed were climate change, habitat destruction and mismanagement, disturbance, photographers, dog walkers, game birds, inbreeding and the media. Each of these factors on their own would pose a serious threat but they have combined to sound the death knell of the adder across much of Britain.

Climate change

In terms of the adder's long-term survival, the greatest threat facing it and all our wildlife is climate change. The adder has continued to evolve over time, adapting to a wide range of environmental threats but the speed with which our climate is changing means it now faces unprecedented challenges. The adder is one of the most versatile reptiles on earth, occurring further north than any other snake and having a wider distribution. This should mean that it is well placed to adapt to our warming world but as so often happens with climatic impacts, the picture is much more complex than it first seems. In the last hundred years, the average global temperature has increased by about one degree Fahrenheit. This should benefit cold-blooded species like the adder which relies on basking in the sun, particularly in the early season, to become active and has to hibernate underground to survive the winter. However, global heating has also resulted in a range of other changes which are far less beneficial to the adder, particularly increasing levels of disturbance and predation.

The most obvious impact of a changing climate on adders can be seen in their activity levels and the amount of time they spend hibernating. Adders traditionally hibernated underground from November to March, a strategy designed to enable them to survive a cold winter, but with warmer weather they are now increasingly active during these months. In 2015, for the first time ever, the adder was observed in every month of the year in the National Park De Meinweg, in the southern Dutch province of Limburg. On 28 December 2015, Peter Keijsers saw an adder and reported it in an article in *Nature Today*, a website publishing topical stories written by Dutch biologists. His claim made headlines throughout Europe, with many herpetologists confirming the trend. Although a sighting in December is exceptional, especially so late in the month, in recent years more and more sightings of adders have been reported early and late in the season. Following Keijsers' sighting, in 2019 adders were also confirmed as being active in every month of the year in Britain by the herpetologist Nigel Hand. He said in an article in the *Guardian*:

> I've seen adders in every month of the year except December, but have had reliable reports of them being active then in Wales. Adders have already been recorded as being seen throughout the year in a national park in the Netherlands, so I have no doubt they are now active throughout the year in Britain as well.[26]

In 2019, Britain became the first country in the world to declare a 'Climate Emergency', reflecting the damage being done to our biodiversity by climate change. The adder provides a good indication of how many species will be impacted by milder and wetter winters and rising temperatures in the autumn and spring. Records have shown that adders are becoming more active for longer into the season and also emerging from their hibernation sites on warm winter days. As a result, it has been calculated that adders now emerge from hibernation up to a month earlier than they did 100 years ago. While this has some advantages as they get 'up to temperature' earlier in the season, it can also prove fatal if the milder weather is followed by a cold snap as has happened

An adder basks in the early spring sun. Climate change and lack of genetic diversity is now also threatening adder populations. (Author)

in recent years in Britain. Emerging from hibernation in winter will also mean greater contact with people, dogs and other predators, leading to increased disturbance at a time when they are particularly vulnerable because they are sluggish and bask in the open. Where adders occur on sites that are used by the public for recreation, a further complication is that there are often no restrictions in place because it will be assumed that adders will be hibernating.

Another direct impact of climate change is the submergence of hibernation sites as rivers flood more frequently. Adders carefully choose high, dry ground for winter hibernation and pass the time underground in sites like old tree roots, rabbit burrows and rodent tunnels. These are selected so they are deep enough to be immune from the cold weather above ground and can withstand occasional flooding. However, they are often not deep enough to protect from water penetration when a site is underwater for long periods. As a result, increased flooding in winter is likely to mean that adders which have not chosen to hibernate in an air pocket are much more likely to drown. This like many of the other impacts of climate change on adders urgently needs more research if we are to understand how future global heating will impact on the species.

As the adder is on the edge of its range in Britain, it is an important indicator of climate change. In 2013, Natural England carried out research into how different species

Young adders shelter beneath a stone. They are very vulnerable during their first few weeks of life. (Roger McPhail)

In terms of its future long-term survival, the greatest threat to the adder and all our wildlife is climate change. The adder, despite being cold blooded, will lose under many climate change scenarios. (Markus Spiske)

are responding to changes in our weather.[27] This included launching a series of report cards showing the winners and losers among Britain's amphibians and reptiles. The report cards showed that the smooth snake, natterjack toad and common toad with the right climatic conditions could potentially 'move northward gaining a larger habitat'. By contrast, common lizards, smooth newts and adders were projected to lose 'under many climate change scenarios, but they may expand in Scotland'. The report card was updated in 2015 showing even stronger evidence about how climate change is affecting Britain's biodiversity with adders again projected overall to lose as a result of the changes.

Habitat destruction and mismanagement

If climate change poses one of the greatest future threats to adders, in the past 80 years it has been habitat destruction that has been the single biggest factor in their decline. Much has been written about the wildlife habitats that have been destroyed during this period by agricultural intensification, house building, industrial development, road construction, moorland mismanagement and urban sprawl. However, it is still staggering to think that since the Second World War, Britain has lost 98 per cent of its lowland raised bogs, 97 per cent of its wild flower meadows, over 200,000 miles of hedgerows, half of its ancient woodlands and 75 per cent of its heaths.

The adder has been particularly affected by these land use changes because it has complex habitat requirements, needing safe hibernacula as well as the right vegetative structure for mating, moving and feeding. As adders are extremely faithful to traditional sites, once a population loses a critical part of its habitat requirements they rarely, if ever, return. It is not just the loss of habitats that has had such a dramatic impact on Britain's dwindling adder population but also their fragmentation and degradation. In Make The Adder Count, many of the 90 per cent of sites with ten or fewer adult snakes were isolated or overgrown, meaning adders there had no suitable habitat to move to if they felt threatened or their remaining habitat was destroyed. This makes it vital that positive land management is carried out to benefit the species and corridors are created, wherever possible, to connect existing adder sites.

Many adders are killed each year by the destruction of their hibernacula, particularly by heavy machinery involved in forestry operations and other changes like land drainage, habitat 'improvement', landscaping and burning for driven grouse shooting. The government's Forestry Departments work closely with conservation organisations to identify adder sites, but some hibernation sites are still not recorded, particularly on private land. In the case of upland habitats like moorland and coastal grassland, adder numbers are often determined by how

In the past eighty years habitat destruction has been the single biggest factor in the decline of the adder. (Andrey Kirsanov)

sympathetic land managers are to the species. Many upland moors, including large areas of our national parks, are managed for red grouse which are ground nesters, laying between six and 12 eggs in a grass-lined hollow in April or May. Adders will predate red grouse chicks if they come across them so conflict can occur, especially where other prey items are in short supply. Gamekeeper Simon Lester, who ran the Langholm Moor Demonstration Project in southern Scotland until 2018, stated:

> Predation of grouse chicks is an on-going concern ... I saw an adder with a grouse chick's head in its mouth. Looking at the size of the chick—which looked about four days old, with its wing feathers just forming—and the size of the adder's head, I thought: 'You've bitten off more than you can chew, old sport.' I just had to watch as, with a lot of huffing and puffing and backward motion, the chick slowly disappeared bit by bit until, eventually, only its white feathery feet protruded from the fully distended mouth of this stretched and distorted viper.

Although adders are tolerated more than birds of prey on upland moors, it seems likely that many gamekeepers would not share Lester's sporting view of an adder killing a grouse chick and would take measures against them to protect their birds.

In the north of its range, the adder is more closely associated with grouse moors where it is often persecuted because it will take grouse chicks. (Roger McPhail)

The author Malcolm Smith in his 1951 *New Naturalist guide to British amphibians and reptiles* recorded as many as 17 adders being killed by a gamekeeper with a single shot. The levels of persecution suffered by adders on upland estates is not known and needs monitoring, but this is difficult to do, especially on private land. However, if the record of many gamekeepers in relation to birds of prey like hen harriers is anything to judge by, adders are probably killed illegally in large numbers each year. Despite this the adder continues to be found on upland moors, no doubt helped by the fact that it poses no threat to adult red grouse. In 2020, Langholm Moor was purchased by a public trust following the largest ever community buyout in the south of Scotland, so there at least the adder should have a secure future.

Disturbance

Contrary to its image in the mass media, the adder is a shy and secretive snake which whenever possible avoids interaction with people. An adder's well developed senses will often enable it to detect the approach of people long before they both come into contact with each other. As a result, it will have ample opportunity to slither away, so that all most people ever see of them is a tail disappearing into the undergrowth. On other occasions, their cryptic camouflage will serve them well so that most people will walk right by an adder without even knowing it.

Despite adders avoiding contact with people and being expert at escape, there are times in the year when they are sedentary and therefore much more vulnerable. The most important of these is when they emerge from hibernation in the spring and bask to increase their body temperature. Often in late February and early March on sunny days adders can be seen basking right out in the open not far from their hibernacula. Adders will even bask along the edge of busy footpaths almost impervious to the people walking by. While this is undoubtedly the best time to see them, it is also the period when they are most vulnerable to disturbance.

Often sluggish following being underground for so long during the winter, adders rely almost totally on blending in with their background to prevent them from being spotted. If threatened or alarmed they can show an impressive turn of speed most of the year but during the spring they will often brazen it out or move away very slowly. As a result, more adders are killed during March and early April than at any other time of the year. The other time when adders are vulnerable is when they are moving between hibernation sites and their summer feeding grounds when people out walking can come across them. Although this always results in a spate of adder scare stories every summer in the media, the impact of disturbance on populations is probably less than it is during the spring.

The adder is most vulnerable to disturbance when it emerges from hibernation in the spring. (Author)

Public pressure or disturbance was the number one negative factor reported in Make the Adder Count, surveyors recording it in nearly half of the 260 sites visited (see Box 8). In the survey a wide variety of activities were recorded as impacting adders including mountain biking, off road vehicle racing, rambling/hill walking, horse riding, cycling, photography and especially dog walking. Public pressure can take many forms, some being transitory and having little long-term impact on local populations while others can, if persistent enough, result in adders moving away from sites, being killed or dying. Continual public pressure makes them more vulnerable to being killed by predators, while in extreme cases stressed adders, subject to ongoing disturbance by people, will not reproduce or feed, leading to a lingering death. In most cases it is a minority of irresponsible people who cause all the problems although in the case of some activities like rambling and hill walking the disturbance is often accidental.

Disturbance is deemed to be a key factor limiting the adder's spread in Scotland even when suitable habitat is available. Unlike in England and Wales, adder habitats are more widely distributed in Scotland, but the species' recorded distribution is still

An adder senses danger. Disturbance is a growing problem, particularly by irresponsible dog walkers whose dogs can end up getting bitten. (Author)

fragmentary and their numbers have declined greatly since the Second World War. Research carried out at different sites near Loch Lomond showed that adders were only found where they could avoid human interference, the researcher Christopher J. McInerny believing this could be used to explain their distribution across the country. He stated, 'Elsewhere, adders are found in nature reserves, on private land, on islands, and in remote, little visited areas. Where they are (rarely) found in proximity to humans, this is usually the result of local tolerance.'[28]

One site where adders have held their own but which is also very popular with people is Hounslow Heath in the west of London. A designated Local Nature Reserve and a Site of Metropolitan Importance, the 80 hectare site is owned and managed by the London Borough of Hounslow. Composed of lowland heath, dry grassland, wood, scrub and meadows, the site is surrounded by houses and buildings including a mosque and is close to Heathrow Airport. Despite its very urban setting, the heath is one of the most important sites for reptiles in London, supporting adders, grass snakes, 'common' lizards, slow worms and amphibians. However, Hounslow Heath is also very popular with people exercising their dogs, runners, walkers and – if Trip Advisor is to be believed – after dark drug dealers, drunks and doggers. The fact that adders occur on the heath is well known locally and as a result the local community has become very protective of them led by the Friends of Hounslow Heath. Following a high-profile case of an adder biting a man there in 2017, signs were put up on the heath in the area where the adders occur telling people about their presence and asking them to keep their dogs on a lead. The signs also warned that the taking, injuring, killing or disturbing of snakes is prohibited under the Wildlife and Countryside Act 1981. Since the signs have been put up, people and adders have co-existed peacefully.

While Hounslow Heath represents a good example of what can be achieved when a local community takes pride in its adders, in many sites disturbance from people is a key factor pushing the species over the brink to extinction. The authors of the Make the Adder Count survey concluded:

> There is very little quantitative data relating to the effects of disturbance on reptiles and the dramatic increase in the reporting of public pressure, such that nearly half of sites are now negatively affected by public pressure, suggests this factor needs urgent investigation, both to assess its impacts on adder populations and to identify potential measures to reduce these impacts.

Hounslow Heath represents a good example of what can be achieved when a local community takes pride in its adders. (Friends of Hounslow Heath)

BOX 8: MAKE THE ADDER COUNT

Make the Adder Count was published in 2019 and is the most comprehensive survey of the adder's distribution and conservation status ever undertaken. The survey recorded adders at 260 sites spread across Britain, surveyors being asked to provide information about the site including the amount of suitable habitat present and how isolated the site was. Those carrying out the survey were also asked to record any threats to the colony.

The most frequently reported threat to adders was public disturbance, affecting 48 per cent of sites. The report stated, 'The fact that public pressure was reported to negatively affect almost half of the 260 sites suggests this is an issue which needs urgent attention, to quantify its effects on adders and, if necessary, to identify effective means of reducing this pressure.'

Habitat management was the most frequently reported positive factor, affecting 28 per cent of sites and conversely the second most reported negative factor affecting 22 per cent of sites. The authors commented:

'Greater effort must be made to raise awareness among land managers of the habitat requirements and activity patterns of adders. Currently

A group of adders. Make the Adder Count was the most comprehensive survey of adders ever undertaken. Published in 2019, it showed that if current rates of decline continue in 15-20 years time the species will be extinct across much of its range in Britain. (Roger McPhail)

> around half of management operations negatively impact adders; if these negative impacts can be replaced by positive impacts, e.g. by protecting hibernacula and avoiding use of heavy machinery during active periods, this could contribute significantly towards halting population declines.'
>
> Habitat fragmentation was the third most frequently reported negative factor affecting 17 per cent of sites. The authors of Make the Adder Count said:
>
> 'Just over 80% of the small population sites were <1km from another site and 16% of them reported habitat fragmentation as a negative factor, while none of the large population sites were reportedly affected by habitat fragmentation. This suggests maintaining connectivity, especially between small populations, should be a priority.'

Photographers

When it comes to the adder, some photographers will go to extraordinary lengths to get the 'perfect shot'. Over-zealous photographers are seen by herpetologists as a growing problem at certain sites as they will often go back repeatedly. In some cases, snakes are then caught and kept in captivity so that they can be manipulated for the perfect shot. In 2011, a group of four men were seen by a member of the public taking adders from the Forest of Dean in Gloucestershire. The sighting made the national news and the police investigated the theft but did not arrest anybody. It is likely that every year there are similar episodes which do not get reported or make the news and that photographers are largely responsible.

Despite a minority of irresponsible individuals, photography does have an important role to play in identifying individual snakes (see Box 9) and helping all of us appreciate the beauty of adders. In 2016, an adder workshop was run by ARG UK as part of a series on the 'Vanishing Viper: Priorities for Adder conservation'. A wide range of people involved in adder conservation were asked to assess the importance of different human-adder interactions to get a better picture of how public pressure is affecting the species. In the case of disturbance from photographers, most recorders believed it was not a major issue and the numbers involved were probably small. However, at some sites it was considered to be an increasing problem, delegates expressing fears about photographers sharing locations online leading to greater disturbance. It concluded that while most wildlife photographers acted responsibly, better education and a code of practice was needed.

Male adders fighting, the type of shot photographers will go back many times to capture. (Roger McPhail)

THE SECRET LIFE OF THE ADDER

An adder uses the bracken for camouflage. They are often a trophy species for photographers. (Author)

Most photographers know not to disturb adders and to be guarded about revealing sites. However, a minority of over-zealous ones continue to break the rules, often posting images online and naming sites. This both increases disturbance and is unnecessary as there is a plethora of good photographs available. In order to reduce the demand for more images, the ARC have introduced a free library of adder images on flickr, many of which feature in this book.

Dog walkers

Another form of growing public disturbance considered by the workshop was dog walkers and the highly controversial subject of adder bites on dogs. Trying to manage sites for both adders and dog walkers is a big challenge for all conservation bodies and land managers, one made more difficult by the number of adder scare stories appearing in the media each year. While there is a lot of anecdotal evidence that irresponsible dog walkers are now adversely impacting adder populations at many sites, there has been no systematic monitoring of this form of disturbance.

Despite what the mass media may have us believe, adders biting dogs is a rare occurrence, snakes always trying to escape if possible. However, dogs have a far better sense of smell than people and a natural sense of curiosity which often leads them to seek out snakes. Female adders have special cloacal glands at the base of their tails and when in season give off a strong scent to attract a mate which can be detected by dogs. Male adders can also attract their attention particularly when basking in the spring. Even when they escape underground, dogs can detect adders, typically growling and scratching at the ground with their tail and ears up.

As dogs are much faster and more agile than people, it means they are more likely to come across an adder in the open. The snake, feeling threatened, will then defend itself with the result that the dog sometimes gets bitten on the nose or face. What the media coverage of adders biting dogs does not reflect is the number of dogs that kill adders each year. Some breeds on seeing a snake will simply be curious while others will actively hunt the adder and kill it. It is likely that the number of adders being killed each year as a result of dog bites is far greater than the other way around, most dogs recovering after having been bitten by the snake. There is no quantitative evidence of the number of adders killed each year by dogs, but it is likely to be on a par with deliberate persecution by people. While dogs biting adders does not make a good story on a slow news day, adders biting dogs does generate easy headlines and business for veterinary practices.

An adder detects a dog approaching. Uncontrolled dogs off leads are liable to get bitten but will also kill adders. (Author)

Many vets in areas where adders are common will each year treat a number of dogs which have been bitten, although in most practices the number of cases is unlikely to amount to double figures. Vets like any other business need to advertise so most have a website which will usually include pages on the symptoms resulting from a bite and what to do if your dog is bitten. Some vets, especially those in hotspots like the New Forest, will also issue adder warnings telling people with dogs to be vigilant where adders are present. These warnings often get promoted in the media or used when the news of an adder bite reaches a local reporter. However, vets, like the media, should have a responsibility to not only report on bites but also to reinforce messages about adders being fully protected by the law and the need to conserve them. Sadly, these messages are often demoted to a few sentences at the end of the article or web page, if they are included at all.

Sites used by both adders and dogs require active management to ensure that both species are kept apart as much as possible, particularly in the spring. This is usually achieved using interpretation boards telling visitors about the presence of adders and voluntary codes of conduct which ask dog owners to keep their pets under control. The statutory Countryside Code also clearly states that people must keep their dog under effective control to ensure that it stays away from wildlife. Despite both signs and the Countryside Code, a minority of dog walkers regularly flout the rules which can bring them into conflict with adders.

One of the adder sites where they are trying to strike this difficult balance is Kinver Edge, a beauty spot and area of heathland on the border between Worcestershire and Staffordshire, managed by the National Trust. Adders in the Midlands have undergone a catastrophic decline, the species now being extinct in the nearby counties of Nottinghamshire and Warwickshire. The 600 acres of coniferous forest and heath at Kinver Edge is a remnant of the Mercia Forest and has a small population of adders so the National Trust decided to manage the site to increase their numbers. This included clear felling coniferous woodland to restore the heath and gating off sensitive areas to allow cattle grazing. However, this proved to be controversial with some horse riders so following protests the National Trust scaled back its plans. The site is also very popular with dog walkers who come in large numbers to the area to exercise their pets. As a result there has been an ongoing dispute between the National Trust and a small minority of dog owners who believe adders threaten their pets.

In 2014 a dog was bitten at the site by an adder and had to be treated at a local vet, leaving the owner, Chris Poole, with a £1,500 bill. As a result, in a media interview he warned other dog lovers and parents visiting the site to be alert, stating 'It is a beautiful place and I don't want to scare people or put them off going but I think they should be aware. Many walkers I have spoken to have seen adders basking on the pathways and if children are playing in the area a bite could be fatal.' However, the owner went further and accused the National Trust of releasing adders into

The adder has undergone its most drastic decline in the Midlands and is now extinct across much of Middle England. (Roger McPhail)

the area for 'conservation reasons' and stated that other dogs had also been bitten. Despite the National Trust denying that adders had been released or that any other dogs had been bitten, the rumour took hold and spread among local dog walkers. Persisting over the years, the accusation culminated in another owner, Teresa Parkes, submitting a Freedom of Information request to the National Trust in 2019 accusing them of releasing snakes and stating 'This is of serious concern as it affects walkers, children, dogs and horse riders. The number of dogs bitten by a snake in recent time [sic] has increased dramatically.'

The National Trust in its reply again denied it had released any snakes at the site and declared it had no plans to do so, stating:

> Adders live here naturally, and they are just one of the many rare species that depend on lowland heath. We aim to create the right conditions for these endangered animals to be able to survive, to stabilise the existing populations and prevent localised extinction of these native species .... Kinver Edge is also a much loved beauty spot and green lung for many people, so we also manage it for walkers, cyclists and horse riders to enjoy. With responsible behaviour there is no reason why people and their pets shouldn't be able to enjoy this space as they always have alongside the native wildlife that calls it home.

The National Trust's desire to manage Kinver Edge for adders and the conflict with some dog owners perfectly illustrates the challenges facing the conservation movement at sites where both occur. In an attempt to better understand their habitat requirements and what to do to conserve them, the National Trust has carried out radio tracking of a number of adders at Kinver Edge. This showed that in summer the

Dog bites are rare but attract a lot of sensational media coverage which has given the species an undeserved image problem. (Nick Dobbs)

adders ranged over larger areas of the heath in search of feeding grounds but were otherwise confined to a small part of the site. The complaint was made despite the National Trust placing interpretation boards on all gates to the site stating that the area contains adders and asking dog walkers to keep their animals on a lead from the beginning of March until the end of July.

The National Trust championing the species is welcome, but they face significant challenges in trying to strike the right balance. The reason that dogs get bitten on Kinver Edge and other similar sites is because irresponsible owners ignore the warning signs and let them run free. If the National Trust and other conservation bodies are to better manage any future conflict between dogs and adders, they need to be able to enforce their own rules or exclude dogs from areas where snakes occur.

Game birds

Most people see pheasants when out walking, their abrupt, explosive flights and raucous alarm calls when flushed making them a very visible part of the landscape. They also come across them in the autumn when millions of birds are released and they rush out in front of oncoming traffic, many ending up as road kills. The general impression is of a harmless, inane bird, whose showy iridescent gold and chestnut-brown plumage and erratic behaviour brightens up the British countryside.

What most people don't appreciate is that from being innocuous, pheasants are in fact highly predatory birds which will attack and kill adders on sight. Although the snake will try to defend itself, the pheasant nearly always comes off best in any encounter because the adder's bite is unable to penetrate the bird's thick mantle of feathers. On seeing a snake, the pheasant will dance around it while aiming powerful pecks at its head and eyes. Even if the adder is able to dodge the pecks, the commotion will usually attract other pheasants who will then work together to attack and kill the snake. Even if they can escape their tormentors, many fully grown adders are badly injured and often slither away only to die a slow and lingering death. Those that do survive battles with pheasants often show a wide range of injuries from being blind and deformed to having 'puncture' wounds on their bodies. Most young and baby adders do not escape and are swallowed whole.

The common pheasant is not native to Britain but originates in China and East Asia where they inhabit a wide range of semi-wooded habitats from temperate scrub to humid tropical forests. They are also found from sea level right up to 4,000 metres in the Himalayas and Western China. Also known as the ring-necked pheasant in the United States, they have been widely introduced across much of the rest of the world because of their value as a game bird for the shooting industry.

In Britain, over 60 million game birds are released each year, in 2018 it being estimated that 49.5 million pheasants and 11.7 million partridges were released by estates and shoots into the countryside. According to the not-for-profit campaigning group Wild Justice, these numbers have increased ten-fold over the last 45 years. Pheasants are captive bred by over 300 game farms across Britain or imported into the country, in 2019 the League Against Cruel Sports calculating that over 27 million game birds were imported from factory farms in France, Spain, Portugal and Poland. They are then all released at the start of the shooting season, which runs from 1 October to 1 of February, and are shot for 'sport', the Game Farmers' Association claiming that the industry is worth more than £2 billion a year. This figure is contested by conservation groups who claim it is not independently verified and does not take account of many wider environmental costs. Many wealthy and influential people also shoot, from the ex-Prime Minister David Cameron to the former cricketer Lord Botham. This together with the strength of the shooting lobby probably accounts for the fact that the industry remained completely unregulated until 2020.

The fate of over 60 million birds released each year is that only about a third end up getting shot, the rest dispersing widely into the countryside and many dying of disease, being killed on the roads, starving to death or ending up as prey themselves. The sheer number of game birds released each year not only threatens adders but also

The fate of over 60 million game birds released each year is that only about a third end up getting shot, the rest dispersing widely. Many end up dead on the roads or roam the countryside. (Author)

An open wound on an adder caused by a game bird. They will attack adders on sight often killing or injuring them, the adders bite failing to penetrate their thick mantle of feathers. (Roger McPhail)

maintains artificially high populations of carrion crows, foxes and other predators. Game birds can also carry ticks harbouring Lyme disease, a bacterial infection which can be a serious threat to human health if not treated. In addition, the lead ammunition often used to shoot them can accumulate up the food chain, threatening to poison both wildlife and people.

Conservationists believe the release of such vast numbers of non-native birds into the British countryside is having a severe adverse impact on many sensitive wildlife sites and species including adders, a claim refuted by the shooting industry. However, in 2020, following a legal action by Wild Justice, the government stated that a new licensing regime would be needed from 2021 for releases of common pheasant and red-legged partridge in Special Areas of Conservation and Special Protection Areas and that a 500m buffer zone would need to be created around release sites. The announcement was made just days before the government would have been taken to the High Court by Wild Justice in a case they were widely expected to lose.

It remains to be seen how effective the new licensing system is, but conservationists believe a 500m buffer zone is nothing like big enough. Research carried out in the United States showed that female pheasants had a home range of 28 acres and male pheasants 21-30 acres.[29] There is also a lot of anecdotal evidence that they disperse widely once released and can travel over a mile to forage. To conserve the adder, the licensing system must include a sufficient buffer zone to ensure that no game birds can get on to adder sites or any other sensitive wildlife reserves.

Inbreeding

As adders have become rarer and confined to smaller, more isolated sites, herpetologists have begun to see increasing problems associated with inbreeding. Before the Second World War, adders often occurred on large, unbroken areas of heathland and other suitable habitats which over the intervening years have not only reduced considerably in size but have also become increasingly fragmented and isolated. As many adder sites across Britain are now surrounded by roads, development or intensive agriculture, snakes have become increasingly marooned in closed populations. This was shown by the Make the Adder Count survey published in 2019 which found that many of the sites with ten or fewer adult adders were separated from other areas of suitable habitat. As a result herpetologists have become increasing concerned about genetic abnormality in small adder populations.

A study carried out in southern Sweden of an isolated population of adders found that due to their highly competitive mating system a few males fathered most of the young each year.[30] This resulted in a smaller number of baby adders, a higher proportion of deformed or stillborn young, a lower degree of genetic variability and a higher genetic similarity among individuals. In contrast when the authors introduced males from other areas into the study population, the number of deformed young was greatly reduced.

More recently, a major study of genetic and demographic vulnerability of UK adder populations found that although there was no loss of genetic variability at sites, there was a striking level of relatedness.[31] The authors found a high proportion of individuals to be related at a level equivalent to that of half-siblings or sharing a parent. This was put down to a high level of faithfulness to a site and adders not being able to move between locations. However, the fact that male adders will mate with several partners does help to offset the risk of inbreeding in some closed populations.

While the study concluded that the British adder population is still at the moment genetically viable, it also showed that the potential is now high for future inbreeding in the remaining small and isolated adder populations. As a result, snake experts from the Zoological Society of London together with Natural Earth and Oxford University are carrying out a survey of the genetic diversity of adders by taking DNA swabs. The study is focussing on the Midlands where the decline in the adder population has been most marked. The initial results already point to an increasing number of adders exhibiting deformities, from crooked spines to deformed heads, as well as a lower number of young.

The Amphibian and Reptile Conservation Trust is also building up a 'Reptile Genebank' by asking people to send in sloughed or shed skins of snakes from which DNA can be extracted. It is hoped that the Reptile Genebank will be a resource

A solitary adder surveys its world. As adders now occur on increasingly small and isolated sites, inbreeding and genetic abnormalities are being increasingly recorded. (Ray Hamilton)

that can be used for long term studies into the effects of population isolation. Early predictions from this monitoring indicates a similar trend to that shown in the Swedish study with small, isolated populations over time becoming less viable due to an increasing number of deformities and infertile snakes.

The media

No other species of British wildlife gets as much negative, misleading and damaging publicity as the adder. Every year there is a spate of snake scare or 'horror' stories, many of which paint the adder as an aggressive species when the opposite is true. In contrast few, if any, mention that the species is in danger of becoming extinct across much of Britain. So when it comes to conserving the adder, responsible reporting in the media has a critical role to play.

Put the word 'adder' into the search engine Google, click on 'news' and it brings up thousands of results, many of which are reports of adders biting dogs and people, the headline writers and journalists often deploying highly sensationalist language to make their point. Some of the headlines in 2020 including the following:

> Dog walkers beware - adders are being spotted, and their bite can be fatal to pets. *Bournemouth Echo* 12 April 2020

> Adder at Gloucestershire beauty spot prompts police alert: here's what they look like and what to do if you're bitten. *Gloucestershire Live* 6 May 2020

> SNAKE HORROR Toddler, 2, rushed to hospital after being attacked by snake during walk in woods. *The Sun* 20 May 2020

Warning after dog needed two blood transfusions after snake bite. *Bristol Live* 20 May 2020

SNAKE BITE: Berriew mum feared for her leg after adder poisoning. *Powys County Times* 2 July 2020

Boy, 3, 'paralysed' by adder bite at country park and left 'in excruciating pain'. *Daily Mirror* 14 July 2020

Warnings as deadly adders filmed in sand dunes day after boy, 3, left 'paralysed'. *Daily Mirror* 15 July 2020

'EXCRUCIATING PAIN' Boy, 3, in hospital and unable to walk after being bitten by adder during picnic. *The Sun* 15 July 2020

Dad's warning after son, 3, left 'paralysed' by adder bite at country park. *Berkshire Live* 18 July 2020

Three year old boy left temporarily paralysed after being bitten by an adder in a park in Surrey. *ITV News* 28 July 2020

Woman suffers 'indescribable' pain after snake bite at park. *Eastern Daily Press* 9 September 2020

Dog 'unrecognisable' after being bitten by adder in UK holiday home garden. *Daily Mirror* 14 September 2020

Terrier's head swells to twice normal size after adder bite. *Dorset Echo* 18 September 2020

Massive snake spotted at Devon beauty spot. *Devon Live* 22 September

GRAPHIC IMAGES: Vale Vets in Dursley treat dog's adder bite. *Gloucestershire Gazette* 23 September 2020

Vets warn owners as dog battles 'biggest wound they'd ever seen' after adder bite. *Metro* 24 September 2020

An adder senses someone approaching. When it comes to the media, no other species of British wildlife generates such unprovoked fear or lurid tabloid headlines as the adder. (Author)

You have trawl through over 50 lurid headlines (many containing words like 'deadly', 'paralysed' or 'graphic' to make their point) before you come across one article on the plight of the adder, the *Coventry Observer* running a piece called 'Adders could be facing a risk of extinction across Britain' on 9 July 2020. For a species which is declining rapidly across Britain, the number of stories is out of all proportion to the threat posed by adders and undoubtedly gives rise to the impression that the species is much more common and dangerous than it actually is. It is a sad paradox that as the adder has disappeared from the countryside, so the number of scare stories about them in the media has increased, fuelled by editors demanding sensational stories, clickbait journalism and people with mobile phones recording their experiences.

While it is true that some adder bites can be extremely painful and cause serious complications, particularly in small dogs, the elderly and the young, most are not that serious. In the case of many stories reported in the media, the dog or person bitten usually makes a full recovery as anti-venom is now readily available. The fact that no one has died in over 40 years in Britain is a testimony to the success of hospitals in treating adder bites. It is also a reflection of how rare the species has now become in a crowded island of over 60 million people where there is increasingly little space left for wildlife.

Stories about adders biting dogs make up the majority of snake horror stories and are particularly prevalent in the local press and the tabloids during the summer. According to the Amphibian and Reptile Conservation Trust, approximately 100 dogs are bitten by adders every year in comparison to around 50 to 100 people. When you consider that there are an estimated 9 million dogs in Britain with a quarter of households owning one, that means that 0.0001 per cent of dogs are bitten by adders each year, a minuscule number.

If you read the articles, it becomes clear how sensationalist some of the reports are. Typical is a report in the *Dorset Echo* on 18 September 2020 with the headline 'Terrier's head swells to twice normal size after adder bite'. According to the paper, the 'snake drama' began when a couple, Ray and Denise Peck, visited a holiday house in Studland on the Dorset coast with their pet terrier Chloe. The article clearly stated that at the site 'adders are such a regular feature that there are signs up

Two male adders 'dance' for the attention of a female. The adder receives more negative media coverage than any other species (Roger McPhail)

warning of their presence.' Ray acknowledged this in the article telling the reporter 'We've stayed in the house before and we saw an adder in the garden last year, so we realised very quickly what had happened. It's pretty much adder central down there.' He went on 'The garden had just been cut back and we think the adder has maybe been dislodged while that work was going on.' Many fair-minded people would conclude from this that the dog loving couple should have chosen somewhere else to stay. However, the paper instead decided to splash on the agony of the dog instead of the poor judgement of the owners.

At the top of the article was a picture of Chloe with a very bruised face taken at the vets, the journalist Ben Williets telling *Dorset Echo* readers, 'The poisonous snake bite saw Chloe's head swell to twice its normal size, with black bruising eclipsing her face. She could barely open her mouth to breathe and her eyes had completely disappeared.' Later on in the article, Catherine Rose, the senior nurse at the Vets Now pet emergency clinic in Bournemouth, was quoted as saying 'If we hadn't given the anti-venom then there was a chance Chloe wouldn't have made it through, partly because she is just so little and the bite was so severe.' It took *Dorset Echo* readers to point out to the paper in the online comments section that the adder was a protected species and they only bite when they feel threatened. Encouragingly of the four comments on the article, two took the paper to task, one read, 'The *Dorset Echo* should state that adders are a protective [sic] species. They only bite when threatened. Their habitat has reduced through human development so contact with pets does result' and another tellingly stated 'Agreed. We wouldn't want a bunch of irate dog lovers going on a snake-killing rampage.'

Another case on 9 September 2020 was reported by the *Eastern Daily Press* with the headline 'Woman suffers "indescribable" pain after snake bite at park'. The article was about 76-year-old retired head teacher Angela Morris who was bitten by an adder while out walking her dog Igor at Holt Country Park. Miss Morris, who had driven to the park from her home, told the journalist Stuart Anderson:

> It was a hot day during the lockdown, soon after we were allowed to drive somewhere for a walk. I hadn't been walking long because I have arthritic knees when I felt a prickling all around my big toe. Then the pain started so I got back to my car as quickly as possible and drove home. I rang 111 and they sent an ambulance, and they drove with sirens blazing to Queen Elizabeth Hospital, where I was kept overnight.

The article was accompanied by some graphic images of Miss Morris's swollen right leg complete with a large blood blister. While there was no denying the pain that Miss Morris felt, what made her really cross was the lack of warning signs, she telling the reporter. 'I'm so angry that they won't take it seriously enough to put up a sign

As the adder cannot defend itself it is reliant on herpetologists and conservationists to make its case. The snake from the Gruffalo trail at Fineshade Woods in Northamptonshire. (Author)

to stop anyone else going through what I've been through.' So Anderson put her accusation to the council who in an unusual move defended their management of the park, if not the right of snakes to be there. The council representative said:

> We have six advisory signs and posters in and around the amenity area where visitors arrive and periodically update our social media channels with information about adders and other wildlife that can be found at the park. As adder bites are so rare, indeed this is the first case brought to our attention in over 20 years, we consider our current signage and awareness efforts to be sufficient for keeping visitors informed, and have no plans to increase signage in the area. We wish the woman in question a speedy recovery and hope she will be able to visit us again soon.

As the adder is facing local extinction across much of Britain it deserves a much more balanced press that it gets. However, in recent years more stories have appeared about the conservation of the species in the media, particularly reports about the threats it is facing. For example, in the autumn of 2020 an article by the author about the threat posed to adders by game birds was run by the *Guardian*, the story being widely picked by other papers including the *Daily Telegraph* and *the Times*. However, there is still considerable bias in large sections of the press who insist on seeing any adder bite

An adder approaches a froglet, one of its favourite prey. If the adder detects movement it will strike. (Roger McPhail)

An adder eats a frog. There is now widespread acceptance that adders need our protection and that means giving them a fair press. (Roger McPhail)

as a 'sensational story'. In 2020, the *Daily Mail* and the *Daily Mirror* ran four stories and the *Sun* three about adder bites, all going into great detail about 'life threatening injuries' to dogs and children, one article even describing adders as 'deadly'. In all of the cases despite the bites being painful, each of the victims made a full recovery. None of them mentioned that the adder was threatened and only one of the stories featured a comment from a representative of a conservation organisation. Reporting on adder bites may be legitimate journalism in the eyes of some editors who would argue that it helps to warn people of their presence, but it needs to be balanced by stories about their conservation.

Human persecution

One consequence of their bad press is that adders have been killed relentlessly throughout our history, a persecution which continues to this day. In the past, killing adders was something to be boasted about, the snake catcher Brusher Mills proudly claiming to have killed thousands of snakes in his lifetime. In Scotland records clearly show that the reduction in the range of the adder over the last century and a half can be attributed to deliberate human persecution. Historical records showed that when 60 acres of ground at Loch Moss on the Solway were reclaimed in the early 1860s, a staggering 2,400 adders were killed.[32]

Following a long history of persecution, the adder was finally fully protected in 1981 after which high profile cases of killing adders became rare, perpetrators knowing that they could be prosecuted. However, many herpetologists believe that adder persecution still frequently occurs but goes unreported, the law merely meaning that the problem is out of sight and out of mind. When it comes to successful prosecutions, adders fare even worse than birds of prey, there having been no cases brought since the passing of the 1981 Wildlife and Countryside Act. Even where there is evidence there still seems a marked reluctance to prosecute.

In September 2019, a columnist on the *Stroud News and Journal* called John Light published an opinion piece on wasps and adders.[33] Having just discovered a wasp's nest in his garden, he wrote:

> It will not be there long, as its demise has instantly been planned. Loving nature and with a countryside upbringing, wasps are creatures without a known purpose and worse still without a known predator, unless you include the fearless aggressive Mrs Light. They do their evil deeds with total impunity. Perhaps adders come into the same category.

Stroud is home to a tiny population of adders which are present in a country park, where they are in danger of extinction. Light berated the fact that adders could still be found sunning themselves on 'warm Cotswold banks' near his home where they lived their lives 'not threatened by another living creature' (this is patently wrong as adders have many natural predators). Light recounted with pride how his father had 'killed 13 in one summer and early autumn without seeking them out. He simply encountered them and then often equipped with billhook, axe or pickaxe acted in appropriate fashion.' Light concluded that this was the best way to deal with adders, his column indirectly inciting their killing and being written 'on a sunny autumn morning when our countryside is at its best. No wasp or adder will stop me enjoying it to the full.'

What is interesting about Light's opinion piece is that all the twelve online comments it attracted utterly condemned his view (in comparison most of the *Stroud News and Journal*'s online articles attract no comments at all). One reader stated, 'Just to point out, for anyone considering copying the actions of your father. Adders are protected under the 1981 Wildlife and Countryside Act, which makes it an illegal offence to kill them.' Another said, 'Are you advocating destruction of adders, Mr Light? It's illegal. And stupid. Adders are fabulous creatures and don't trouble people unless disturbed. So leave them alone. And please stop writing such

Despite adders being fully protected by law, large numbers continue to be illegally killed. (Author)

unutterable drivel. SNJ take note … this has got to stop. This column is truly awful. And lacking in paragraphs. As usual.' However, it took another reader for the paper to see sense. They wrote:

> Adders are beautiful and wonderful creatures. We need to be thinking of how best we can protect them, not discussing past persecution. It is a rare treat to see an adder. They are very shy and won't bite unless disturbed. They are not as dangerous as portrayed – no one has died from an adder bite in the UK for over 50 years. As others have pointed out it is illegal to kill adders. It's very disappointing that this material has been printed. I look forward to a positive adder article and/or apology.

As a result of the criticism, of Light's column, the *Stroud News and Journal* were stung into issuing a response. In October 2019 they ran an article written by Dr Angela Julian, coordinator of the Amphibian and Reptile Groups of the UK and Jennifer Gilbert, Back from the Brink Cotswolds community engagement officer. Julian and Gilbert decided to avoid criticising Light in person and instead they wrote a passionate piece about the need to conserve adders (see Box 10). Despite this in April 2021 an adder was deliberately killed in Stroud, the dead snake being found by a member of the public who stated that it had been repeatedly hit. Although the incident was reported to Gloucestershire Police and an appeal made in the paper to find the perpetrator, no one was prosecuted. Julian condemned the killing and stated 'We are working hard to safeguard and protect the tiny populations of this timid and secretive snake that still remain on the Cotswolds, some numbering only a few individuals, before they too disappear forever from our landscape. These particular animals were well known to the Stroud Town Council rangers, who had been studying and carefully monitoring them over a number of years. Therefore it is particularly painful to lose such a well-loved animal in such a violent and unnecessary manner.' The killing was also condemned by Stroud Council, Councillor Simon Pickering, the Chair of Stroud District Council Environment Committee, saying 'We were shocked and saddened to learn about the cruel and heartless killing of an adder – one of our most vulnerable native species.'

If the public views expressed by Light on adders are becoming less acceptable in our more enlightened times, many adders are still killed each year by dog owners, gamekeepers and people with an irrational fear of snakes. It speaks volumes about our attitude towards conserving adders that in the forty years since the 1981 Wildlife and Countryside Act was passed that neither Light nor anyone else has ever been prosecuted for killing them.

A dead adder. Despite being fully protected by law, there has never been a prosecution for killing an adder. (Roger McPhail)

BOX 9: ADDER HEAD MARKINGS

The herpetologist Sylvia Sheldon has been studying adders in the Wyre Forest in Worcestershire for over thirty years. Her pioneering work there has shown that it is possible to identify individual adders using their distinctive head markings because they are unique to each snake. Sheldon initially sketched adders in the field but found this was time consuming and it was difficult to

Research carried out by the herpetologist Sylvia Sheldon has shown that the adder's head pattern is unique and can be used to identify individuals. (Author)

capture all the detail. So, instead, she turned to photography as an easier and more accurate way of identifying snakes.

By using long lenses, Sheldon could photograph snakes without getting too close to them, helping to keep disturbance to a minimum. However, she found it was not always easy to make out the detail on the head as it was sometimes hidden or obscured by vegetation. This made it difficult to distinguish between individuals with similar head patterns. So to identify individuals, Sheldon split the head pattern into three separate parts – the apex of the zigzag, the inverted V on the head and the pattern along the eye line.

If two adders had similar head markings, Sheldon looked at the snake's platelets on the top of its head, the shape of the zigzag and the 'side panels' or scales along its head. By comparing each of these three parts, she was able to accurately identify individuals. Sheldon also discovered that sloughed skins, if whole, were just as good as photographs for identifying snakes.

Sheldon has collected hundreds of photographs of adder heads over the years in her notebooks, proving that each pattern is unique. She also recorded the sex, age, colour, home range and dates when they were seen. By identifying individual snakes, Sheldon was able to follow their movements, discovering much about their ecology in the process. She was also able to accurately evaluate adder numbers at sites by ensuring there was no double counting.[34]

CHAPTER 5

Conserving Adders

.....it biteth like a serpent, and stingeth like an adder.

Proverbs 23:32

At the current rate of decline, the adder is predicted to be extinct across much of Britain in the next 15-20 years, a damning indictment on our ability to conserve one of our most high profile and charismatic species. Despite the conservation movement's best efforts, it has for too long been fighting a losing battle to halt the decline. Given the scale of the threats which the species now faces, much more needs to done to highlight its plight and come up with solutions which will enable the adder to increase in numbers and maintain its range. The stark reality is that unless something changes to stop its decline future generations will only be able to see adders at a very small number of sites or in captivity.

There are nearly 350 national nature reserves designated by the government across Britain but not one single reserve has ever been specifically designated to conserve the adder. (Kieren Ridley)

In comparison to the help given to other species, the adder has never been given the attention it deserves, despite being listed as a Priority Species in the Biodiversity Action Plan (BAP). The UK government is rightly proud of being the first country in the world to draw up a BAP; published in 1994 it lists 1,150 species and 65 habitats which are priorities for conservation action. It has also enshrined in law a legally binding target to halt species loss by 2030. There are nearly 350 national nature reserves designated by the government across Britain and many local reserves managed by local authorities. However, not one single reserve has ever been specifically designated to conserve the adder by government, its statutory nature conservation advisors or local authorities. While many nature reserves run by government and organisations like the National Trust, RSPB and the Wildlife Trusts are managed sympathetically with reptiles in mind, their habitat requirements can be incompatible with other high-profile species. For example, at chalk grassland sites designated for their botanical interest, keeping the turf very short and clearing much of the scrub is the management priority, despite this being bad for snakes.

There is a complex number of reasons why we have failed the adder. Making the case for conserving a venomous snake will never be easy, especially when so

Female adders emerge after the males in the spring. Despite the adder population being in dire straits, it is still not too late to save it if we act now. (Ray Hamilton)

138 THE SECRET LIFE OF THE ADDER

many people mistakenly believe it is dangerous, have pet dogs or simply dislike snakes. Adders have specific habitat requirements and unlike some amphibians are difficult to relocate so this makes their conservation considerably more challenging. Inevitably there will be a small number of bites every year which will always provide lurid stories to those parts of the media who insist on viewing adders as aggressive animals. Predation and persecution by people are continuing problems, many predators of adders like crows having increased considerably in recent years. The number of reptiles in Britain is also very small and this is reflected in the membership of organisations like ARG UK who lack the money, influence and reserves of big conservation organisations like the National Trust and the RSPB. Unlike 'popular species' like avocets or hedgehogs, adders also lack high profile friends and are rarely held up by politicians as being a priority for conservation. However, despite these challenges there have been some promising projects in recent years which could still help to save the species.

The following is a ten-point action plan which, if implemented, could yet save the adder and help return the snake to its former range over the next decade.

1. Protect in law all remaining adder sites

While the adder is fully protected in law under the 1981 Wildlife and Countryside Act (WCA), the legislation is now increasingly out of date and is not being enforced. In 2021 the Environment Act was passed establishing a new legal duty to halt the decline in biodiversity by 2030. This could help the adder if it protects in law all remaining adder sites.

In 1991, the WCA was amended to make it illegal to intentionally kill and injure adders or to offer them for sale but not take them from the wild. The penalties were also increased to a fine of £5,000, or six months' imprisonment. Despite this, not a single prosecution for killing adders has been brought since the act was passed over forty years ago. One reason is that perversely the law still allows for their destruction where this is the result of an otherwise lawful activity that 'could not reasonably have been avoided'. So it is legal to kill or injure an adder as a result of development where a 'reasonable effort' has been made to translocate them.

The 260 sites where adders were recorded by Make the Adder Count cover many different locations, occurring on nature reserves, public and private land. While adder sites occurring on nature reserves are supposedly protected in law, many small adder sites have no protection or their protection is weak and can be easily overridden. For example, recent reforms to the planning system in favour of development and major infrastructure projects like HS2 mean that many more sites are now under threat.

This is despite every public body having a duty under the BAP to not only conserve adders but where possible to restore or enhance their populations or habitats.

In 2016, Tony Gent, the Chief Executive Officer of the ARC, addressed the issue of protecting adders in law as part of the Vanishing Viper series. He questioned whether much of the legislation now in place is addressing the right threats to adders or being enforced. Gent called for a range of actions including new legislation to protect habitats, improved site designation, greater protection through the

New legislation is now needed to protect adder sites if the species is to be saved. (Roger McPhail)

planning system, an enhanced biodiversity duty and the better targeting of so called 'agri-environment' schemes to benefit adders. In the years since Gent made those recommendations the adder population has continued to significantly decline and the species is now on the brink of extinction across much of Britain. So it is now imperative that his proposals are acted on and adder habitats are fully protected as part of the governments legally binding target to conserve the species by 2030. In particular the law needs to protect not just the snakes themselves but also sites where adders still occur, focussing on known hibernacula.

2. Create viable adder populations in every county/region

While conserving existing adder populations is vital, we also need to restore them to areas from where they have been lost. The most effective way of doing this would be to reintroduce adders to locations where they have formerly been present, particularly the Midlands, as the species is now considered to be extinct in Warwickshire, Oxfordshire and Nottinghamshire.

The last confirmed sighting of an adder in Warwickshire was in 2004, records prior to this date indicating that the species was confined to a very few sites in the county. Despite subsequent monitoring of all potential sites over the next 14 years, no adders were found, so in 2018 it was officially declared extinct. In Oxfordshire, the species hung on another decade, their last known location being the Warburg nature reserve in the Chilterns belonging to the Berks, Bucks and Oxon Wildlife Trust. Here a very small population of three or four snakes were present until 2014, the trust going to great efforts to conserve the species. However, disturbance and predation by pheasants, kites and buzzards meant that in 2015 the last adder in Oxfordshire was killed, so the species in now considered extinct in the county.

In Nottinghamshire, the species was officially considered extinct in 2016, no reliable reports being received of any sightings for over ten years. However, a new conservation project here is being used to bring the adder back from extinction. The People's Trust for Endangered Species (PTES) and Nottinghamshire Wildlife Trust conducted a feasibility study in 2016 with a view to reintroducing the species. The report stated that, 'The historic loss of adder habitat, particularly from the Sherwood area, is believed to have driven the species' long term decline, while the last known population was likely extirpated by scrub encroachment on isolated clearings within a forestry plantation.'

Following a review of adder translocations and the practice of reintroducing reptiles, a computer simulation model was used to 'determine the feasibility of adder reintroduction and assess factors likely to influence its success.' The model suggested that over 70 adult adders would need to be reintroduced to ensure a viable long-term population. According to PTES its success will depend on the 'behavioural response to translocation and the

Adders moved to a new location. Translocating adders is controversial, and the results have been mixed. (Ray Hamilton)

suitability and extent of habitat, rates of juvenile mortality and female reproduction'. The report concluded that 'There is a clear case for adder reintroduction to Nottinghamshire, with potential to serve as a case study for adder conservation.'

In 2019, PTES announced that it was beginning the reintroduction project and it hoped to return the species to the county within five years. The Trust also said it would be drawing up a bespoke plan based on guidelines drawn up the International Union for the Conservation of Nature about whether captive breeding or translocations were an 'acceptable option'. However, the high-profile nature of the project has raised some concerns and it is still to be seen whether or not the reintroduction will work.

The success of previous translocation projects has been mixed. A study written up in 2020 of over 500 translocated reptiles showed very low levels of recapture after three years, at half of the sites surveyed no translocated reptiles being found at all, the authors concluding that the animals had either died or migrated away from the dispersal site.[35] Another translocation of over 40 adders to Hounslow Heath in Greater London in 2000 was more successful, a number of gravid females being found in 2016.[36] The project co-ordinator concluded that good partnerships with site managers and appropriate management of the receptor site were the key to a successful translocation.

Translocation, using captive-bred snakes or ones from sites earmarked for development, is a controversial way to create new adder populations in those areas

A translocated adder eats a frog. Reintroductions despite being controversial probably offer the best hope of helping adders recover their former range. (Roger McPhail)

where they have become locally extinct. However, where suitable habitat is present and the reasons for the original demise are well understood, it offers the best hope of helping adders to recover their original range.

3. Teach 'Adders are Amazing!' in schools

In an effort to improve the adder's image among the public, in 2018 a campaign called 'Adders Are Amazing!' was started by ARG UK headed by the television naturalist Iolo Williams. To promote it, local children took part in a Saint David's Day Parade through their local town holding aloft a giant adder or 'Gwiber' in the style of a Chinese dragon. Wales is one of the snake's last remaining strongholds, adders still being common on the coast although inland they have declined markedly. At the launch, Williams said, 'Adders do suffer from a very bad image problem. But if you look at snakes in films, they're all evil characters. That's such a shame. But if you look at an adder, the male and female look very different. They have these beautiful blood red eyes, this zig zag brown or black down the back. And they are amazing things.'

Local school children in St David's hold aloft a giant adder or 'Gwiber' in the style of a Chinese dragon. Teaching school children about adders as part of a GCSE in natural history could help reverse the image problem associated with the snake. (ARG UK)

The campaign aims to challenge negative public perceptions about snakes, the organisers stating, 'Adders have been persecuted over many centuries, and without a significant change in the way in which communities and the wider public view the adder, there is no desire or impetus to conserve it.' The Adders are Amazing project could form part of a Natural History General Certificate of Secondary Education, a qualification which the government is currently considering as part of the national curriculum. Teaching children about natural history in all our schools would make a major contribution to reversing the 'image problem' associated with adders and other 'unpopular' species like spiders and wasps.

The adder as an integral part of our history and our only venomous snake is also surely worthy of celebration in its own right. The United Nations has designated the 16 July each year as World Snake Day to raise awareness of the issues surrounding snakes from persecution to protection. To help promote adder conservation in Britain the government could adopt this day or designate 1 March, Saint David's Day, a national adder day. Together with teaching projects like Adders are Amazing, celebrating snakes could help to change the fortune of the species, encouraging many more people to learn about adders.

4. Recruit a new generation of adder champions

It is one of the paradoxes of adder conservation that the more the plight of the adder gets publicised, the more potential disturbance is brought to bear on the remaining sites where it is still found. This is the reason why so many herpetologists are extremely wary of publicising the species and they keep sites where it occurs secret. The challenge is to get people to love adders while by default not encouraging more people to visit sites where they are already struggling to survive. Establishing a network of 'adder trails' at well publicised sites where people are encouraged to visit could help, in the process taking the pressure off other smaller and more sensitive locations.

A high-profile project which has taken a pioneering approach to getting people to appreciate the species is the adder trail at the RSPBs Minsmere reserve. Every spring, signs are placed around the reserve encouraging people to look for adders basking in the open or camouflaged in the leaf litter. The trail is also publicised on the reserves website and blog. The signs encourage people to 'tread lightly and approach slowly as adders are easily disturbed by vibrations and sudden movements.' Minsmere attracts over 90,000 visitors every year and the project has been really successful at encouraging people to not only look out for adders but also appreciate their beauty. Those walking the adder trail in the spring also get the opportunity to take closeup photographs of the snakes. To date, despite the adder trail at Minsmere being walked by tens of thousands of people, no one has been bitten, a shining example of how people and adders can happily coexist.

A series of adder trails like the one at Minsmere could help take the pressure off other smaller and more sensitive locations. (RSPB)

The challenge in the future will be managing access to some large sites where adders are common while giving the maximum protection to the remaining smaller sites where they are still found. To help, adder champions should be recruited with the objective of establishing adder trails similar to the one at Minsmere at selected sites across Britain. A drive to recruit a new generation of adder champions in schools, colleges, universities and from across society could transform both the image and the fate of the species. The champions could be trained by staff from herpetological or conservation groups, like the volunteers participating in the Back from the Brink projects. A carefully managed series of adder trails managed by adder champions would showcase the species and act as a magnate for those wishing to see or photograph them.

Another very good public awareness project which could be replicated elsewhere is the New Forest Reptile Centre. The centre run by Forestry England is located in Lyndhurst in Hampshire and houses a unique collection of all our native British frogs, toads, lizards and snakes including the adder. The centre includes live wildlife cameras and a discovery trail, a circular walk through the surrounding woods where people can see a range of reptiles. The New Forest Reptile Centre is an excellent example of a public education project that if expanded to other parts of Britain could introduce many more people to the wonder of snakes and recruit a new generation of adder champions.

The adder would also benefit from a high-profile champion who is willing to make the case for its conservation to government. Prince William has in recent years established himself as a conservation and climate change champion, in 2020 becoming the President of the British Trust for Ornithology and launching the Earthshot Prize to find solutions to some of the world's most pressing environmental problems. Following in the footsteps of his father and his late grandfather, he has criticised the killing of endangered species abroad and promoted conservation at home across the royal estate. In 2020 he starred in *Prince William — A Planet for Us All*, a television programme produced by Silverback Films (see Box 7). The Sandringham and Balmoral estates support adder populations but both locations also host big royal shoots, 'wild' pheasants and partridges being shot at Sandringham and grouse and deer at Balmoral. Prince William and his wife Catherine are keen shots who believe that shooting and conservation are compatible, both regularly participating in country sports. However, in recent years there have been increasing calls to rewild the royal estate. One way of demonstrating this would be to ensure a sufficient buffer zone is in place to prevent game birds coming into contact with adders and for Prince William to become a champion for the species, like he is for endangered wildlife abroad.

An adder consumes a mouse. The species needs new high profile adder champions like Prince William who can champion its conservation. (Roger McPhail)

CONSERVING ADDERS

5. Report sensational and negative stories to the press regulator

When it comes to media publicity about the adder, much of the current coverage of the species is not balanced, fair or accurate. Despite adder bites being an extremely rare occurrence, every year they are turned into sensational stories which are perpetuating the myth that adders are dangerous. The sad irony is that as the species has declined, so negative coverage of it has increased in the form of clickbait journalism. While the media have a right to report on adder bites, they should also have a responsibility to put the tiny number of bites into context and say why we need to conserve the species. This particularly applies to local papers and national ones like the *Daily Mail*, the *Sun* and the *Daily Mirror*. Press standards in the UK are regulated by the Independent Press Standards Organisation (IPSO) for the newspaper and magazine industry. IPSO ensures that newspapers and magazines follow the Editors' Code and investigate complaints about breaches of the code. The Editors' Code includes an 'accuracy' clause which states the press must not publish inaccurate, misleading or distorted information or images, including headlines not supported by the text. Based on this definition, much of the reporting of adders stories in local papers and the national press may be in breach of the code.

As the adder cannot defend itself, it is reliant on herpetologists and conservationists to make its case but given the sheer number of headlines each year, this is a big challenge. However, bringing more cases to IPSO's attention may help to stop some of the more sensationalist or biased adder stories. Any breaches of the code would also have to be investigated which could be a deterrent to those editors who run unbalanced or sensational news stories without thinking through the wider implications for a species struggling to survive.

The media needs to balance reporting of adder bites with conservation of the species. (BBC)

6. Expand the Back from the Brink projects to the whole of Britain

Back from the Brink and its Welsh equivalent Connecting the Dragons are projects which offer real hope for conserving Britain's dwindling adders if the money can be found to extend them nationally. Launched in 2017 with funding from the National Lottery and other charitable trusts, Back from the Brink has been developed by Natural England and Rethink Nature. Uniquely, it brings together a partnership of seven conservation charities: Amphibian and Reptile Conservation Trust, Bat Conservation Trust, Bumblebee Conservation Trust, Buglife, Butterfly Conservation, Plantlife and the RSPB. Its aim is to 'save 20 species from extinction and benefit over 200 more through 19 projects that span England; from the tip of Cornwall to Northumberland.'

Rockingham Forest in Northamptonshire is a former royal hunting forest created by William I which is now composed of a series of woods managed by Forestry England. Famed for its red kites, several of the woods still support adder populations which were thought to be declining but there was little hard data. In response, the Roots of Rockingham Forest project was set up, one of five Back from the Brink projects targeting adders. It aims to assess the adder population across the area and take action to conserve them. To do this, volunteers were firstly trained to locate and

Back from the Brink are projects which offer real hope for conserving Britain's dwindling adders if the money can be found to roll them out nationally. (Roger McPhail)

map the adders, surveying both existing and former sites across the forest. The results surprisingly revealed a larger than expected population of adders, the organisers concluding that they formed 'part of one of Eastern England's most important reptile communities'. As a result of the survey work, several hibernacula have been safeguarded from forestry operations and habitat management work has gone on across the forest to benefit the species.

Back from the Brink provides a powerful example of what can be achieved when the conservation movement works together with funding, clear objectives and trained volunteers. The problem is the lack of budget and political will to extend the project across Britain. To save the adder it is essential that the statutory nature conservation agencies now make the political case for conserving adders to government and give the species the priority it deserves under the BAP.

7. Ban dogs from all sites where adders occur

Despite a lot of media coverage to the contrary, adders biting dogs remains a very rare event. The adder is not aggressive and will never attack a dog, but they will defend themselves if provoked or molested. Unfortunately, due to their natural curiosity, dogs are the pet animals most likely to be bitten but adder bites are rarely fatal, most dogs making a full recovery. However, uncontrolled dogs threaten conservation efforts at many sites like Kinver Edge in the Midlands.

A dog's behaviour towards other animals is largely determined by how responsible their owners are, many dog owners when visiting wildlife sites abiding by the rules. However, a minority of irresponsible owners let their dogs roam freely, even when there are signs asking them to keep their pets under control or on a lead. The experience of trying to conserve adders at Kinver Edge shows that despite very clear signs too many dog owners simply ignore the rules and allow their animals to wander all over the heath. This significantly increases the chances that they will come into contact with adders and get bitten. It is a similar story throughout Britain where dogs are allowed on sensitive wildlife sites.

As there are nine million dogs in Britain, a minority of irresponsible owners still results in far too many dogs out of control which has led to increasing calls in recent years for them to be banned from nature reserves. At Kinver Edge, a lot of visitors to the site are dog owners who nearly all drive to get there and then exercise their pets. At the site the voluntary approach has clearly failed and tougher measures will be needed if the small adder population there is to have any chance of recovering. The same is true of most of other small sites which support adders but are also popular dog walking locations.

When it comes to enforcing the law protecting adders, many nature conservations organisations feel powerless and so revert to the voluntary approach like the National

Trust do at Kinver Edge. In comparison, when it comes to the impact that dogs have on livestock farmers there are very strict rules, the Dogs (Protection of Livestock) Act 1953 stating that if a dog worries a sheep, the person can be charged with a criminal offence and fined up to £1,000. The act defines the term 'worrying' very broadly, including attacking and chasing livestock which can cause injury or suffering. It also includes being 'at large' where livestock are present, classified as not being on a lead or otherwise under close control. In exceptional circumstances under the Animals Act 1971 farmers also have the right to shoot a dog, a point reinforced in the Countryside Code which states they may not be liable to compensate the owner.

Given the scale of the decline of the adder over the last decade, there is now a strong case for dogs to be banned on all sites where snakes occur, if not more broadly on all nature reserves. This needs to be backed up by similar powers to those in the Dog Act 1953 so that conservation agencies and other land managers feel that they have the power to enforce the ban. Although any ban would be controversial with dog owners, some would support it such as the television naturalist and ARC Patron Chris Packham. A high-profile dog lover who presents programmes like *Me and My Dog*, Packham has long recognised that dogs need to be kept apart from sensitive wildlife like adders. In his 2018 People's Manifesto for Wildlife, Packham proposed that dogs should be banned on all nature reserves, commenting 'I simply don't get the dogs on nature reserves thing. At all. The ambiguity of 'under control' is nonsense. We should just end it – no dogs.'

Given the scale of the decline of the adder over the last decade, there is now an overwhelming case for dogs to be banned on sites where snakes occur. (Lehmannsound)

8. Make it illegal to release game birds within a mile of adder colonies

The uncontrolled release of over 60 million pheasants and partridges into the countryside each year now threatens the adder's future survival at many sites near shoots across Britain according to the herpetologist Nigel Hand. In 2019, he stated, 'The adder is on the brink of extinction in many sites across Britain. In the Malverns where I live and across many other sites it is the uncontrolled release of millions of pheasants by shooting estates which is pushing it over the brink.' As a result, in 2020 the campaigning organisation Wild Justice took the government to court over the issue, the Department of the Environment, Food and Rural Affairs (DEFRA) agreeing that the release of game birds into the British countryside should require a licence.

The move was widely welcomed by many herpetological groups, Jim Foster, the Conservation Director at the Amphibian and Reptile Conservation Trust, commenting:

> The notion that reptiles might be harmed by some gamebird releases has long been a concern for ARC due to our own observations, and through liaison with volunteers, scientists and other land managers. A licence is needed for the release of many non-native species, and some native ones, even in low numbers. It has

The game bird licensing scheme must take the 'precautionary approach' and ensure that it is illegal to release birds within at least a mile or 1.6 km of any adder colony. (Zonda)

always seemed incongruous that permission was unnecessary for the release of tens of millions of pheasants.

The licensing scheme currently only covers Special Conservation Areas and Special Protection Areas under European law, but these designations do not cover the vast majority of known adder sites. Most of the 260 sites monitored as part of the Make the Adder Count survey are spread widely but thinly throughout the British countryside with the exception of the Midlands. These sites are well known to local herpetologists and other wildlife enthusiasts so to help conserve the adder it is essential that the DEFRA licensing scheme be extended to cover them.

After release, pheasants disperse widely into the countryside, many ending up on roads where they are killed by cars or providing easy pickings for predators like crows and foxes. However, others come into contact with local wildlife, reptiles in particular being vulnerable to predation by the birds. In a study in the US, reared pheasants dispersed 1.6–3.2 km from their release point,[37] British pheasants dispersing similar distances. So in line with the precautionary approach, the licensing scheme should be extended to include all known adder sites. To keep game birds and snakes apart it should be a legal requirement to have a buffer zone of at least one mile or 1.6km between a shoot and any known adder colony.

9. Build a nationwide network of adder corridors by rewilding

The loss of suitable habitat, particularly from agricultural intensification, industrialisation and urban development, has been a major factor in the decline of the adder. In Britain today there are no real wilderness areas left, even the remotest areas of Scotland being impacted, not least by climate change. However, in response to the lack of wilderness there are ambitious proposals to 'rewild' the countryside by organisations like Rewilding Britain, their current projects including pine forests, upland valleys, farmland, private estates, public lands, nature reserves, marine protected areas and coastal community projects.

High-profile projects like Knepp farm in Sussex, Wild Ken Hill Farm in Norfolk and the Cairngorms Connect project in Scotland have received a lot of publicity and show what can be achieved. The adder is a high-profile species and rewilding could have major benefits for the species if it is targeted to benefit existing populations. In particular, rewildling could help to join the many existing small populations through the creation of adder corridors. With 90 per cent of the sites surveyed in Make the Adder Count containing ten or fewer adult snakes, joining together small and scattered populations must now be now a conservation priority, particularly in those areas where the species is on the verge of local extinction.

Rewilding and creating adder corridors could have major benefits for the species if it is targeted to benefit existing populations. (Author)

10. Designate adder nature reserves and fund a new adder conservation programme

Adders occur in a wide range of habitats across Britain with differing degrees of public access which are managed by a number of different organisations. Many are found on nature reserves or other designated sites managed by organisations like the RSPB, National Trust, Wildlife Trusts, Natural England, NatureScot, Natural Resources Wales and the Woodland Trust. Other populations occur on moors, forests, commons, Forestry Department land and Ministry of Defence bases and training grounds. There are also small populations in public parks, golf courses, housing estates and private land. Conserving adders therefore involves dealing with a large number of different landowners who will have varying attitudes towards the snakes found on their land.

When it comes to conserving our declining population of adders, much of the liaison with landowners outside of nature reserves is done by two remarkable charities who have made a major contribution to adder conservation. The Amphibian and Reptile Groups of the UK (ARG UK) are 45 county-based volunteer groups who do the grass roots work involved in conserving adders. Volunteers survey sites, carry out practical conservation work and tell people about the wonders of amphibians and reptiles. Their work is organised by a central coordinator who represents the groups at a national level to government. Locally, ARG UK volunteers liaise with planners, landowners, site managers, conservation groups and the public about adder conservation. It is a mark of their contribution that ARG UK members accounted for many of the Make the Adder Count records which first alerted conservationists to the scale of the adder's decline.

The Amphibian and Reptile Conservation Trust (ARC) was formed in 2009 and is the largest organisation concerned specifically with the conservation of the adder. Employing over 30 full time staff, its aim is to become 'the leading herpetological conservation body working on the UK Biodiversity Action Plan'. The ARC manages many small reserves from coastal dunes to clay pits and woodland to heathland which are home to a wide range of reptiles. As well as conservation, the ARC puts on education and training programmes, influences policy, runs campaigns and collects data. Those wishing to help can become an 'ARC Friend', the organisation having several thousand members. Together with ARG UK, they also organise the Record Pool which collects data on adders and operate the National Amphibian and Reptile Recording Scheme.

Despite all this good work, the conservation of adders is far too dependent on the commitment, enthusiasm and time of a relatively small number of people and volunteers. Given the scale and rate of decline of the adder across Britain, it is sad how little interest has been shown by the government's own nature conservation agencies in England, Scotland and Wales. Despite the adder being a priority species

A group of male adders basking together, an increasingly rare sight. The Amphibian and Reptiles Groups of the UK and The Amphibian and Reptile Conservation Trust have done sterling work in raising the profile of the adder and monitoring the species. (Nick Dobbs)

under the UK Biodiversity Action Plan, the government has singularly failed to take a leading role in its conservation. Of the 224 National Nature Reserves and 4,128 Sites of Special Scientific Interest (SSSI) designated by Natural England, the jewels in the crown of conservation, none have been specifically designated to protect adders. As a result, in 2016, Paul Edgar, a senior environmental specialist in amphibians and reptiles at Natural England, recommended that new SSSIs be specifically created to protect adder sites.[38] However, to date none have been designated. Edgar also recommended the targeting of 'agri-environment' schemes to help adders but so far, no specific programme has been established to benefit the species.

If the adder is not to become extinct across much of Britain in the next 15-20 years, the government now needs to urgently designate adder SSSI's starting with the most vulnerable colonies. In order to encourage landowners to conserve hibernacula and proactively manage habitat, an adder conservation grant should also be introduced

If the adder is not to become extinct across much of Britain, the government now needs to urgently start designating adder Sites of Special Scientific Interest starting with the most vulnerable colonies. (Roger McPhail)

which targets existing colonies and is available to all land managers responsible for their care. Combined, these two measures could form a species recovery programme which begins to stem the decline and helps bring back the adder from the brink of extinction over the next decade.

BOX 10: OPINION: ADDERS IN DESPERATE NEED OF CONSERVATION

This article was written by Dr Angela Julian, coordinator of the Amphibian and Reptile Groups of the UK and Jennifer Gilbert, Back from the Brink Cotswolds community engagement officer, in response to a 2019 column in the *Stroud News and Journal* by John Light about the killing of adders.

We are responding to recent concerns about adders in the Cotswolds. Already extinct in Oxfordshire and Warwickshire, the adder is declining rapidly across Britain. Even in Gloucestershire adders are declining, and many people will go a lifetime not seeing one. As such, they are considered to be in desperate need of conservation action.

A major reason for this is loss and fragmentation of their habitat. As roads and development spread across Britain's green spaces, there are fewer undisturbed spots for our native creatures. Adders also have a number of predators, including crows, ravens and birds of prey, such as buzzards. Even pheasants are a threat, attacking the snakes as they bask in the sunshine.

Despite all the sensational media coverage and lurid headlines, many people will go a lifetime without seeing an adder. (Author)

Ironically, one of the biggest threats to our native adder is people. The systematic and thoughtless killing of adders over hundreds of years has decimated their numbers. Even today, although adders are protected under the Wildlife and Countryside Act (1981) and it is illegal to kill or injure them, we still receive reports of this type of mindless cruelty. The main reason given for this fear is that the adder is venomous. However, far from being aggressive, it is actually a timid and secretive animal.

The venom produced is designed to subdue the small rodents they prey on, not to attack people, dogs or any other large mammal. Unfortunately, occasionally people and dogs do inadvertently stumble across them and can receive a painful bite, requiring medical attention. We therefore recommend that you do not touch or try to pick an adder up, and keep your dog under close control on known adder sites.

The Back from the Brink project Limestone's Living Legacies, aims to redress the worrying declines we are seeing in our local biodiversity, including our adders. By working with local conservation partners including Natural England and Gloucestershire Amphibian and Reptile Group, we aim to help save our threatened species through a major conservation and outreach programme across the Cotswolds.

Bibliography

Bell, Thomas (1839) *A history of British Reptiles* John Van Voorst London

Blyton, Enid (1952) *Animal Lover's Book* Evans Brothers Limited London

Bright, Michael (2006) *Beasts of the field: The Revealing Natural History of Animals of the Bible* Pavilion Books

Cooke, M.C. (1865) *Our Reptiles - A plain guide and easy account of the Lizards, Snakes, Newts, Toads, Frogs and Tortoises indigenous to Great Britain* Robert Hardwicke

Gardner, Emma; Julian, Angela; Monk Chris; Baker John (2019) *Make the Adder Count: population trends from a citizen science survey of UK adders* Herpetological Journal Vol 29, pp. 57-70

Leighton, Gerald. R (1901) *The Life-History of British Serpents and their Local Distributions in the British Isles* William Blackwood and Sons

Morrison, Norman (1924) *The Life-Story of the Adder* Paisley: Alexander Gardner Ltd

McPhail, Rodger (2011) *The Private Life of Adders* Merlin Unwin Books

Prestt, Ian (1971) *An ecological study of the viper Vipera berus in southern Britain* Journal of Zoology Vol 164, pp. 373-418

Smith, Malcolm (1951) *The British Amphibians and Reptiles* The New Naturalist Collins

Stafford, Peter (1987) *The Adder* Shire Natural History

Westwood, Brett & Moss, Stephen (2017) *Wonderland: A Year of Britain's Wildlife, Day by Day* John Murray

References

1. *The Holy Bible: King James Version* (1611) Genesis 3: 1-16 Hendrickson Publishers
2. Leighton, Gerald R. (1901) *The Life-History of British Serpents and their local Distribution in the British Isles* William Blackwood and Sons pp.231
3. Kembridge, Richard (2015) *Cold Blood: Adventures with Reptiles and Amphibians* Random House pp.322
4. Gumbel, Nicky *Bible In One Year* (2019) January 26 Why does God Allow Suffering https://bibleinoneyear.org/bioy/commentary/2060
5. Osbaldiston, William Augustus (1792) *The British Sportsman, or Nobleman, Gentleman, and Farmer's Dictionary of Recreation and Amusement*' J. Stead London pp.6
6. Bell, Thomas (1839) *A History of British Reptiles* John Van Voorst London pp.59-60
7. West, Anna (2017) *Thomas Hardy and Animals* Cambridge: Cambridge University Press
8. Leighton pp.225
9. Hudson W. H. (1919) *The Book of a Naturalist* Hodder and Stoughton
10. Blyton, Enid (1952) *Animal Lover's Book* Evans Brothers Limited London pp.97-98
11. Leighton, pp.223
12. Cooke, A.S. & Arnold, H.R. (1982) 'National changes in the status of the commoner British amphibians and reptiles before 1974'. *British Journal of Herpetology* 6, 206–207
13. Cooke, A.S. & Scorgie, H.R.A. (1983) 'The status of the commoner amphibians and reptiles in Britain'. *Focus on Nature Conservation, No. 3*. Peterborough: Nature Conservancy Council.
14. Hilton-Brown, D. & Oldham, R.S. (1991) 'The status of the widespread amphibians and reptiles in Britain, 1990, and changes during the 1980s'. *Focus on Nature Conservation, No. 131*. Peterborough: Nature Conservancy Council.
15. Baker, J., Suckling, J. and Carey, R. (2004) 'Status of the adder *Vipera berus* and slow-worm *Anguis fragilis* in England'. *English Nature Research Reports Number 546*. Peterborough: English Nature.
16. Gleed-Owen, C. & Langham, S. (2012). 'The Adder Status Project – a conservation condition assessment of the adder (*Vipera berus*) in England, with recommendations for future monitoring and conservation policy'. *Unpublished report*. CGO Ecology Ltd, Bournemouth.

17. Hand, N. (2018) 'The secret life of the adder (Vipera berus) revealed through telemetry' *The Glasgow Naturalist* Volume 27, Supplement. *The Amphibians and Reptiles of Scotland*
18. Wüster, Wolfgang et al. (2005) 'Do aposematism and Batesian mimicry require bright colours? A test, using European viper markings'. *Proceedings. Biological sciences/The Royal Society*. 271. pp. 2495-9.
19. Reid H. A. (1976). 'Adder bites in Britain'. *British Medical Journal*, 2 (6028), pp.153–156
20. Young Bruce A. (2003) 'Snake Bioacoustics: Toward a Richer Understanding of the Behavioral Ecology of Snakes' *Quarterly Review of Biology* Vol. 78 No. 3 pp.303-325
21. Milton, Nicholas (2019) Adders now active all year with warmer UK weather *The Guardian* 6 March
22. Stafford, Peter (1987) *The Adder* Shire Natural History p.9
23. Andrén, Claes (1985) 'Risk of predation in male and female adders, *Vipera berus* (Linné)' *Amphibia-Reptilia* Vol. 6 p.203-206
24. Nash, Darryn and Professor Griffiths Richard (2018) 'Ranging behaviour of adders (*Vipera berus*) translocated from a development site' *Herpetological Journal* Vol. 28 pp. 155-159
25. Alastair Fothergill in conversation with the author October 2020
26. Milton, Nicholas (2019) Adders now active all year with warmer UK weather *The Guardian* 6 March
27. Morecroft, M.D. and Speakman, L. (2013/2015) Biodiversity Climate Change Impacts Summary Report. *Living With Environmental Change*.
28. McInerny, Christopher J. (2014) Habitat preferences of European adders at Loch Lomond, Scotland *The Glasgow Naturalist* Vol. 26 Part 1 pp. 69-74
29. Kuck, Thomas L. (1968) Movements and Behavior of Pheasants During the Breeding Cycle as Determined by Radio-Tracking *South Dakota State University Theses and Dissertations*. 158.
30. Madsen, Thomas & Stille, Bo and Shine, Richard (1996) Inbreeding depression in an isolated population of Adders *Vipera berus*. *Biological Conservation*. 75. pp.113-118
31. Ball S., Hand N., Willman F., Durrant C., Uller T., Claus K., et al. (2020) Genetic and demographic vulnerability of adder populations: Results of a genetic study in mainland Britain. *PLoS ONE* 15(4)
32. Smith, Malcolm (1951) *The British Amphibians and Reptiles* The New Naturalist Collins
33. https://www.stroudnewsandjournal.co.uk/news/17918882.john-light-thank-advice-wasp-problem/
34. Sheldon, S. and Bradly, C. (1989) Identification of individual adders (*Vipera berus*) by their head markings *The Herpetological Journal* Vol. 1. No. 9

35. Nash, D.J., Humphries N. & Griffiths R. A. (2020) Effectiveness of translocation in mitigating reptile-development conflict in the UK *Conservation Evidence* 17 pp.7-11
36. Matthes, Gareth (2016) Adder Translocation Case-study, Hounslow Heath *GPM Ecology*
37. Madden, J.R., Hall, A. & Whiteside, M.A. (2018) Why do many pheasants released in the UK die, and how can we best reduce their natural mortality? *European Journal Wildlife Research* 64, 40
38. Edgar Paul (2016) What is Natural England Doing About Adder Declines? Senior Environmental Specialist (Amphibians & Reptiles) *Natural England Presentation* https://www.arguk.org/info-advice/scientific-and-technical-reports/presentations-from-vanishing-viper-october-2016/296-paul-edgar-site-protection-regulation-and-policy-in-england/file

A male adder shields or guards a female prior to mating. The adder's future now depends on us. (Roger McPhail)

Index

Adders are Amazing 14, 144, 145
Adder's-tongue fern 22
Adder's stone 17, 18
Albino adder 69
Amphibian and Reptile Conservation Trust (ARC) 8, 14, 71, 122, 127, 149, 152, 155, 156
Amphibian and Reptile Groups of the UK (ARG UK) 12, 45, 100, 133, 144, 155
Animals Act 1971 151
Anglo-Saxons 18, 19
Animal Lover's Book 33, 34, 160, 161
Anti-venom 30, 31, 72, 73, 96, 126, 128

Back from the Brink 14, 133, 146, 149, 150, 158, 159
Basking 10, 13, 26, 45, 46, 57, 60, 62, 68, 70, 77, 78, 93, 100, 106, 114, 115, 145, 156
British Broadcasting Corporation (BBC) 38, 96, 97, 148
Bee sting 73
Bell, Thomas 28, 70, 97, 160, 161
Bible 12, 15, 16, 23, 25, 36, 37, 38, 160, 161
Bite 7, 17, 26, 28, 29, 30, 34, 37, 38, 47, 64, 70-73, 83, 89, 97, 113, 115, 117, 120, 123-128, 130, 131, 133, 137, 139, 148, 150, 159, 162
Biodiversity Action Plan 13, 14, 95, 138, 155, 156
Black adder 69, 97
Blackadder (tv series) 69, 97
Blyton, Enid 33, 34, 160, 161

Bright, Michael 38
Brille 57, 59, 64, 74
British Medical Journal 72, 162
British Sportsman, or Nobleman, Gentleman, and Farmer's Dictionary of Recreation and Amusement 26, 161

Cairngorms Connect 153
Chamberlain, Neville 44
Climate change 13, 51, 100 - 103, 146, 153, 162
Cloaca 80, 114
Coloration - see markings
Connecting the Dragons 149
Cooke, Mordecai Cubitt 18, 28, 29, 71, 160, 161
Countryside Code 115, 151

Daily Mail 131, 148
Daily Mirror 124, 125, 131, 148
Dance of the adders 78, 82, 127
Department of the Environment, Food and Rural Affairs 152, 153
Destruction of habitat 7, 44, 45, 100, 103, 104, 111, 128, 141, 153, 158
De Proprietatibus Rerum (On the Properties of Things) 19
Dogs 13, 14, 96, 102, 108, 109, 113-116, 118, 123-127, 131, 139, 150, 151, 159
Dogs (Protection of Livestock) Act 1953 151

Disturbance 13, 85, 100, 102, 106-111, 113, 136, 141, 145
Druids 17

Egyptians 15, 17
Eyes/Eyesight 7, 15, 29, 30, 57, 59, 64, 68-70, 74, 75, 118, 136, 144

Fangs 15, 26, 34, 69, 70, 71, 86
Films 36, 96, 97, 98, 144, 147
Feeding 47, 52, 60, 62, 77, 89, 104, 106, 118
Flooding 102
Forestry Departments/England 104, 146, 149, 155
Forestry operations 100, 104, 141, 150
Foster, Jim 152
Fothergill, Alastair 96, 162

Game birds 13, 14, 93, 94, 96, 100, 118, 119, 121, 130, 152, 153
Game Farmers Association 119
Gardner, Emma 46, 47, 160
Genesis 12, 15, 23, 25, 37, 38, 161
Gent, Tony 140, 141
Gestation period 85
Gilbert, Jennifer 133, 158
Gorgon 48, 49
Grass snake 30, 32, 41, 48, 53, 54, 69, 70, 76, 78, 95, 108
Grouse 44, 104-106, 147
Greeks 15, 23, 48
Guardian 101, 130, 162

Habitat 7, 44, 45, 50, 51, 54, 60-62, 91, 95, 100, 103, 104, 107, 110, 111, 118, 121, 128, 138-141, 143, 144, 150, 153, 155, 156, 162
Hand, Nigel 6, 60, 101, 152, 162
Hardy, Thomas 29, 30, 161
Hearing 74

Hemipenis 80
Hibernation 45, 57, 58, 78, 87, 93, 101, 102, 104, 106, 107, 160
History 15-38
History of British Reptiles 28, 160, 161
Hounslow Heath 108, 109, 143, 163
Hudson, William Henry 32, 33, 161

Ice Age 15, 16
Inbreeding 51, 86, 100, 121-123, 162
Independent Press Standards Organisation 148
Israel 24, 37, 39

Jacobson's organ 75
Jaw 70, 74, 89, 90-92
Journal of Zoology 10, 160
Julian, Angela 46, 133, 158, 160

Keijsers, Peter 100, 101
King Arthur 21, 22
Kinver Edge 115, 117, 118, 150, 151
Kneep farm 153

Land of Israel viper 38
Law 13, 14, 96, 115, 132, 133, 134, 138, 139, 140, 141, 150, 153
League Against Cruel Sports 119
Leighton, Gerald 30, 39-44, 63, 68, 69, 76, 160
Life-History of British Serpents and their Local Distribution in the British Isles 30, 39, 40, 160, 161
Light, John 132, 158, 162

Macbeth 22, 26
Make the Adder Count 12, 13, 45, 46, 104, 107, 109, 110, 111, 121, 139, 153, 155, 160
Markings 9, 54, 65, 68, 94, 135, 136, 162

INDEX 165

Mating 60, 62, 75, 78, 80, 81, 83, 91, 104, 121, 162, 163
McInerny, Christopher 108, 162
McPhail, Roger 6
Media 11, 13, 30, 76, 81, 100, 106, 113, 114, 115, 117, 123, 124, 125, 126, 127, 130, 139, 148, 150, 158
Medusa 29, 48, 49
Mills, Harry 'Brusher' 29-32, 34, 39, 131
Ministry of Defence 155
Minsmere 96, 145, 146
Moorland 44, 60, 104-106, 155
Moss, Stephen 59, 99, 160
Movement 14, 17, 60, 65, 74, 77, 130, 136, 137, 145, 150, 160, 162
Movies - see films
Myths 18, 63-65

Nashawaty, Chris 96, 97
National Nature Reserve 13, 137, 138, 156
National Trust 115-118, 138, 139, 155
Natural History and Antiquities of Selborne 26, 27
Natural England 102, 149, 156, 159, 163
Natural History General Certificate of Secondary Education 144, 145
Nature Conservancy Council 10, 44, 161
New Forest 29, 30, 31, 33, 39, 115, 146
Nine Herbs Charm 19, 56

Odin 19
Osbaldiston, William Augustus 26, 161
Ouroboros 17
Our Reptiles – A plain guide and easy account of the Lizards, Snakes, Newts, Toads, Frogs and Tortoises indigenous to Great Britain 28, 160
Oxford University 122

Packham, Chris 151
People's Trust for Endangered Species 141, 143
Persecution 42, 99, 106, 114, 131-133, 139, 145
Pheasants - see game birds
Photographers 100, 111, 112, 113
Prestt, Ian 6, 160
Predators 13, 51, 60, 65, 73, 83, 87, 93, 94, 95, 102, 107, 121, 132, 139, 153, 158
Prey 18, 30, 37, 38, 52, 60, 64, 70-73, 75, 77, 85, 87, 89, 91-93, 105, 106, 119, 130, 132, 158, 159

Ratcliffe, Derek 10
Reptile Genebank 122
Return of the Native 29, 30
Rewilding 14, 153, 154
Rewilding Britain 153
Roots of Rockingham Forest 149
Royal Society for the Protection of Birds (RSPB) 9-11, 138, 139, 145, 146, 149, 155
Rubens, Peter Paul 48

Saint David's Day 144, 145
Saint Patrick 15, 19, 21
Scent 75, 78, 89, 114
Scholey, Keith 96
Senses 73, 106, 108, 126
Shakespeare, William 12, 22, 26
Sheldon, Sylvia 68, 80, 91, 135, 136, 162
Signs 108, 109, 115, 188, 127, 128, 130, 145, 150
Silverback Films 96, 147
Site of Special Scientific Interest (SSSI) 13, 156, 157
Slow worm 54, 89, 108, 161
Small red viper 41-43, 76
Smell 75, 114
Smith, Malcolm 106, 160, 162

Smooth snake 41, 53, 54, 69, 103
Speed 77, 81, 100, 106
Springwatch 96
Stafford, Peter 78, 160, 162
Stroud 132-134, 158
Stroud News and Journal 132, 133, 162
Summer feeding grounds 60, 77, 91, 106
Sun 13, 26, 46, 51, 54, 78, 100, 101, 106, 132, 158
Sun (newspaper) 123, 124, 131, 148
Symptoms (of being bitten) 28, 71, 72, 115
Snyders, Frans 48

Testes 57, 80
Threats 99 - 137
Tongue 7, 15, 22, 34, 37, 72, 75, 78, 80, 91

Venom 19, 28, 70-73, 75, 77, 82, 86, 87, 89, 159

Veterinary practices 39, 114, 115, 125, 128
Vipera berus 10, 50, 52, 56, 160, 161, 162

Walker, Peter M.P. 10
Wasp (sting) 73, 132, 145, 162
Westwood, Brett 59, 99, 160
White, Gilbert 26, 27
Wildlife Trusts 138, 141, 143, 155
William, Prince 96, 146, 147
Wildlife and Countryside Act 1981 109, 132, 139
Wild Justice 119, 121, 152
Williams, Iolo 6, 8, 144
Woden - see Odin
Woodland Trust 155

Young 17, 26, 27, 41, 42, 52, 56, 57, 63, 64, 85-89, 91, 102, 118, 121, 122, 126

Zoological Society of London 122